Watery Ways

By

Valerie Poore

© 2019 Valerie Poore Rights reserved.

No copying, reproducing, lending, borrowing or sales permitted without the author's consent.

ISBN: 9781980539827

Disclaimer

The events described in this book are true as far as my memory can be relied upon. Certain names have been changed in the interests of discretion, but mostly the people, places and barges are referred to by their real names. As far as possible, all factual information has been corroborated, but I apologise in advance for any inaccuracies. Whatever and wherever they are, they are all part of the rich fabric of these recollections.

For Koos, Jodie and Maryssa

Huge thanks also to all the characters who have been part of this book, especially Philip who, I hope, will forgive my teasing, and Mireille, who I see less of now and miss. Other special thanks are due to my blogger friends for their support and encouragement. Of special note are Anne Marie Klein, Margie Jevons, Maria, a.k.a EL Wisty from Finland, she who calls herself String, and Catherine Marie, known as Gypsy Noir.

TABLE OF CONTENTS

Chapters	Page
1. The beginning of it all	7
2. The water gods	13
3. Village People	25
4. Learning Curves	33
5. March madness	43
6. Spring Fever	57
7. Changes and Developments	71
8. Branching Out	84
9. Local Colour	99
10. Not a Hoop	113
11. On the slips	127
12. Destination Lille	142
13. Loss and Gain	161
14. The beginning of the rest	175
15. Epilogue	193

The Hoop on the Slipway

CHAPTER ONE
The Beginning Of It All

One of the first things you learn when living on a boat is that an awful lot of stuff is going to end up in the water. You also learn that it is a rather special way of life and, looking back, I wish I had come to it much earlier. Being now in what can only kindly be called my middle age, it seems rather late to have started a new love affair, but I can say with complete honesty that is what has happened. What's more, I have thrown caution to the winds with happy abandon and am about to embark on a whole new phase, living by myself on a historic barge in Rotterdam.

Initially, I came to the Netherlands to follow a husband who was in pursuit of one of his numerous career dreams. In South Africa, where I lived before Holland, we had owned our own homes. Not just apartments but real houses, on sizeable plots of land, with big gardens. Shock and disbelief set in when we realised the price of a modest house here could be compared to that of a millionaire's mansion in Johannesburg. We were not going to manage even so much as a lock-up garage on our limited means.

Ever creative, my then-husband started sowing other seeds. "Look at these canals," he said. "Wouldn't it be wonderful to live on a house boat?" he suggested tentatively. Knowing my aversion to all things cold and wet, he was being very brave to even hint at such a possibility. Nevertheless, the seeds found a fertile corner in my mind and I started watching the Dutch *binnenvaartschepen* (inland waterway barges) with some curiosity. As they ploughed their way up and down the rivers and canals I realised I liked what I saw. I became intrigued. Eventually, I became hooked on the idea.

What finally clinched it was the cost of buying a *woonschip* or houseboat. At first we looked at the more conventional *woonarken*, which line many of the canals in most of the big cities. These are, in effect, floating houses. Some of them are built up on the hulls of old barges, but many of them are constructed on concrete bases and remain fixed to their moorings. I have to say that they are very appealing and often come with small gardens, but the price is usually as high as that of a standard house or apartment.

However, we had noticed that in some of the cities there are harbours designated for historic barges, which are also used for living aboard. The appeal of these old cargo-carrying boats is that they can still be used for travel, and the idea of going on holiday and taking my house with me was even more attractive. On investigation, it appeared that we could buy an old flat-bottomed barge for a fraction of the price of a normal house, so, given our love of all things antique and historic, this seemed like a good option. With kids grown and gone and only the dogs and cats to worry about, living space was no longer a major issue. Besides, on a barge you have the whole of the deck to expand onto as well, not to mention being a secure playground for our furry friends.

After several months of searching, we finally found what we wanted at a very reasonable price. The bad news was that to find a permanent mooring for it, we would have to undertake some major restoration work to make it acceptable in one of the historic harbours that we were so keen to live in. The barge we chose had a beautiful hull, but it had been modernised in the seventies and improved beyond repair. It had a kind of caravan structure built over the hold and, even worse, it had the ugliest wheelhouse I have ever seen. Historic harbour or not, this simply had to go.

To cut a long story short, finance for the restoration project was granted after much pleading and grovelling with several banks. Interestingly enough, it is not unusual to have a mortgage for a houseboat in the Netherlands, but the conditions are rather more stringent than they are for a house, and we were newcomers, both working as freelance business English teachers and with no track record – a risk in other words. Following the approval of our loan, and after re-naming it the Kaapse Draai (from a South African expression meaning a life changing U Turn), the barge was accepted into the Oude Haven in Rotterdam to undertake the project. All this was achieved with the help and support of some wonderful people we met in the harbour. Their kindness, humour and oddball approach to life cemented our belief that this was indeed, and at last, The Life.

At the end of February 2000, we were in. Then the problems began. Relations between my husband and I had long been unstable. Now, they deteriorated from rocky to wrecked, and then into total collapse, precipitated mainly by the stress of the undertaking we had embarked on. I retreated from the fray and found myself grateful to be back in South Africa for a six-month spell of work. Its original intention was to help finance the restoration of the barge, but the extended break proved to be too much for an already floundering situation. My husband and I agreed to part.

The problem was, I was still in love with The Life. Depressed didn't even begin to describe how I felt about not living on a boat when I returned to the Netherlands. I even considered not going back at all but, with all my worldly possessions still there, I had little real choice. Then a heaven sent opportunity dropped into my email inbox a few weeks before I was due to fly back.

Before leaving for South Africa, I had spent three months helping one of the harbour dwellers to restore his wheelhouse. It was a labour of love for me as I have a passion for old wood, and the teak timberwork on these old barges was magnificent. In the process of this project, Philip, the owner, became a good friend, and I learnt that he owned three or four barges, all with berths in the neighbouring harbours.

Now word gets around fast in such a small community. It's a bit like the African bush telegraph. People seem to know what's going on like smells on the breeze, so news of my new status had obviously spread, even while I was thousands of kilometres away. To my delight, the email I received was from Philip, and he was offering me The Lifeline – did I want to stay on one of his barges if, and when, I came back?

What a question. Do bees like honey? I decided to give it a try for six months, thinking this should be long enough to see if I could make it alone in the Netherlands.

So it was that, with renewed determination and more than a little eager anticipation, I boarded the plane in Johannesburg last night – at nine-thirty on the twenty-seventh of December 2000, to be precise.

The flight is long, but I am used to it after having made this trip several times before, and I have had plenty of time to reflect on what has led me to this point. Indeed, I am very much aware as I sit in my aisle seat on the great Boeing 747 that this is the first stage of the journey to begin my new life and education in watery ways.

In all possible ways, I am excited about the challenge, but there is a part of me that is nervous and fearful of the decision I have made. Still, it is far too late to turn back now.

The Oude Haven, Rotterdam

CHAPTER TWO
The Water Gods

It is a breathtakingly cold morning as I emerge from the airport at Schiphol. After six months in the sun I am once more unaccustomed to the frigidity of a European winter and my spirits take a momentary dip, only to lift again when I see the broadly grinning face of harbour resident, Mireille. She strides towards me in a curiously attractive manner and hugs me unreservedly. We have been corresponding by email over the months of my absence and it is good to see her again in the flesh. She is in the early stages of pregnancy, but it is invisible as yet and doesn't appear to be affecting her adversely either. Although I am going to be staying with my daughter until I move onto Philip's barge, Mireille's offer of a lift from the airport is just the best welcome I could have.

As we make our way back to Rotterdam, the light filters in from the east and the rosy stain on the horizon spreads up and outwards as we drive, so that by the time we are on the ring road approaching the city, the sky has lightened to reveal a stunning, clear morning. The approach to the harbour is fondly familiar. There is a light dusting of snow on the ground, and, with the sharp bright air, the Oude Haven looks dreamy and indescribably lovely. The tall masts of the sailing barges spear upwards proudly, while clippers rock against traditional *tjalks* with their bows to the quay, for all the world like soldiers in a row.

I have coffee with my friend and we chat quietly until the rest of the world wakes up. Mireille tells me about her PhD, and how she copes with research after morning sickness. We chuckle over the images it evokes, and my mood lifts again. I have a feeling it is going to be all right after all.

A few days later I am looking for Philip to show me my new home. The barge he has in mind is one I've loved and admired from the first. Its name is the Hoop, meaning 'hope' and pronounced the same way, which feels like an omen. It is a graceful old vessel that has never been converted, so the accommodation is still restricted to the original skipper's living quarters behind the wheelhouse. I find Philip on board. He is distinguished by his almost ever present smile. It is wide and dominated by very white teeth. The rest of him varies from tanned to black depending on how much welding he has done when you happen to bump into him. Grinning in greeting, he shows me inside the living area which I have never seen before, and I am totally smitten.

To explain, the families who first owned these old barges lived on them full time, so the skipper would have not just his wife, but all his children on board too. Nevertheless, their boats were their livelihood and their business was carrying goods, so the living area had to take up as little space as possible. From around 1900 onwards, the motor barges had a cabin behind the wheelhouse called the *roef*, which consisted of a built-up area with windows in the side to give both headroom and light. This was great progress as, formerly, the accommodation was below the deck, and such was the sense of comfort that these new models became known as *luxe motors*.

Inside, the cabins were normally panelled with painted wood and beds were built box-style into the curved area of the stern. This then left space for a small salon and kitchen, as well as plenty of cupboard space. Still, it seems inconceivable that whole families lived in these tiny, cramped 'apartments'.

On the Hoop, everything I see now is original. It is so complete I almost can't believe it. All the panelling is untouched, unadulterated and in incredibly good condition; all it needs is a lick or two of paint. There is also extra sleeping space in the *vooronder*, the area below decks in the bows, again with its original panelling. In fact, everything on the Hoop is authentic, even down to its Kromhout single-cylinder hot bulb engine, which is the one it was built with.

I realise in stunned amazement that, although neglected and in need of some major TLC, this barge is a gem. With some careful restoration, it could be worth a fortune – not just as a historic monument, but also as a truly beautiful barge. It has lovely lines and perfect proportions, but best of all it has never been 'messed' with. The wheelhouse is one of the prettiest I have ever seen, although this is the part that needs the most work. No problem for me, since this is definitely my area. After finishing my studies, I spent two years stripping and restoring antique country furniture and have never lost the urge to get my sander out when I see a neglected thing of beauty.

When I mention the Hoop's potential value to Philip, he just smiles. Of course he knows. He has been buying, restoring and selling barges for some time, and is well known for his skill with a welding torch.

He tells me that the old man he bought the barge from never lived in the *roef*; he lived in the hold and used an old wood stove for heating. He'd gradually burnt all the floorboards for fuel, and by the time Philip approached him to buy the barge there were only about four square metres left. Time to go, perhaps? I feel glad and relieved that the *roef* was spared this butchery. The hold is empty now, although the floor has been replaced. Philip has plans to convert it one day and then sell it, but for my part, I hope it's not too soon.

In the meantime, we strike a deal. I will live on it, clean it up, and refurbish the wheelhouse in return for a few months free of rent. I positively beam with contentment. What a pleasure this is going to be.

This brings me back to a key point, though, being that when you live on a barge, numerous objects are likely to end up in the water. They do in my case, anyway.

The reason is only partly because there is a great deal to be learnt about living on board. Bearing in mind that the five months I spent on a barge before my spell in South Africa were with a partner who had a passion for all things mechanical, there are many, many things I don't know. In short, I did the woman thing then, while my husband embraced all those areas which are typically the male domain. This included the fixing of all moving or motorised parts, filling tanks, lighting stoves and checking all exterior necessities, such as ropes, cables and tarpaulins. I must now learn to do all these things myself.

The Hoop has no running water; the toilet is sitting upside down on the bench in the wheelhouse; there is no electric lighting and there are no washing facilities at all. I suppose that some might think this is primitive. On reflection they could be right.

My landlord is charming. A kinder, more generous man you couldn't wish to meet. The trouble is he is also what we call in Afrikaans a *loskop*. The closest and kindest translation for this in English is 'somewhat absent-minded'. In practice, this means that when he says I will have running water, a toilet and a shower by the time I have moved in, I have a strong suspicion it is not going to happen that way.

Undaunted, I prepare to start making it comfortable without these 'mod cons'. I have resumed my work as a freelance teacher since my arrival, so personal hygiene is quite a priority. Luckily, there is a shower I can use in the office building at the shipyard, which is also part of our harbour. I can collect water from there too, and there are always camping style solutions to the toilet problem.

This aside, the first step is to find a door handle for the wheelhouse so that I don't have to use the pair of scissors lying on the *roef* beside it to get in. Effective, but lacking style somehow.

To my great appreciation, Philip appears one morning and presents me with a very nice pair of old brass door knobs, which are slotted into each other for convenience. As we stand chatting on the snow-covered quay next to the barge, I idly start pulling them apart and fitting them back together again. What happens next is predictable I suppose. Walking up the gangplank, clutching my prize by one knob, the other, loosened by my fiddling, slips off and falls without a splash into the water. I gulp guiltily. Philip keeps his smile wide, but there is a set look to it. Ah well, this is only my first offering to the water gods, and I have no doubt there will be others. As for the door, for the moment I will have to go back to the scissors.

The second step in preparing my small but enchanting new home is to organise some power on the Hoop. For me, the only essentials in life are coffee, toast and music, and for all three electricity is a pre-requisite. It is also rather necessary for the sanding machines and the other power tools I will need to start the great fix-up.

Buying long, good quality electric cable is much more difficult than I have anticipated. It seems that anything over fifteen metres comes on a roll without plugs, sockets or adaptors, and is quite pricey per running metre. I can't afford that much, so it takes quite a search through the local hardware stores – a difficulty heightened by the fact that my Dutch is still at elementary level. I haven't got to the "conversations at your DIY shop" in my *Learn Dutch in Three Months* book yet, a time frame I've always felt was a touch optimistic anyway.

But back to the cable. I eventually find one, although I still have to change the plug because when I go, high with expectation, to 'get connected' at the mains box on the quay, I find the sockets are of a type specially designed for mains boxes on quays; not houses. Sigh.

Mireille comes to visit and I ask her where to buy the plug. We discuss the route to the specialist ship's electricians over a cup of strong coffee and *stroopwafels* (syrup waffles), my latest obsession.

Mireille is fast becoming my oracle, encyclopaedia and weather forecaster all rolled into one. Her pregnancy means she is working less on her PhD and has more time to help confused 'wannabe' water rats like myself. She is twenty years my junior, but maturity sits on her calm features like a velvet cloak, and she dispenses both wisdom and quirky jokes with the same expression of wry humour.

After this pleasant interlude I head off for Oechies, the electrician's store she has despatched me to. Creeping round the store, which looks frighteningly like a professionals' supplier and not for amateurs of my lowly calibre, I realise I am being followed by the sales clerk.

"*Wat zoekt u mevrouw?* (What are you looking for?)" he asks me curiously.

I've been hoping I will find the right plug without having to ask for it. I am painfully conscious of my language limitations and don't really know what to say, but now I'll have to try.

"*Ik zoek een* … hmm … uh … *een ding voor mijn elektriciteit.*" ("I'm looking for something for my electricity," is what I hope I've said.)

"*Echt waar!*" (really!) he says with a hint of amusement. We are after all in a shop stuffed full of things for electricity.

Blushing furiously, I point to a plug and make signs to show I want one *als dit* but *groter* (like this, but bigger). The salesman twigs. He kindly leads me to a shelf at the back of the store, and we proceed slowly along the line until I see the blue and white plug I'm looking for. With rather unseemly excitement, I jab at it, and the young clerk picks it up and explains with exaggerated slowness that this one is suitable for 220 volts and not 380 and am I sure this is what I want?

Yes, yes, I nod, and we go to the till, both relieved that we have survived and succeeded in this cross-cultural exchange.

Back at the Hoop, I change the plug. It takes me ages because I don't have the right screwdriver and the thin twists of copper wire keep slipping out of my grasp, but finally I do it and – bingo! I have power on board. At last.

I have bought a kettle and toaster from the second hand stalls at the Saturday market behind the harbour. Mireille and her husband have also donated a radio/CD player they have to spare, so I smugly believe I am all set. Then, horror of horrors, I find that none of the plugs on my critical appliances will fit the socket on my wonderful – now very expensive – cable.

I consult Mireille again. She tells me that in Holland there are different types of plugs for things that need earthing, and these won't fit into the kind of socket I have on my cable. This is news to me, but then everything is news to me these days.

Stubbornly determined not to change my cable or its socket now, I head off again to the market and spend what seems like the cost of a whole crop of brand new appliances on an assortment of adaptors and matching plugs so that I can rig up a system that darned-well will fit my toaster and kettle. Fortunately for me, and everyone else's sanity, it does.

Now, being someone who is quite easily side tracked, and, having ensured that all my life sustaining services work, I start thinking about the fun stuff. Perhaps I should see if my sander works? That would be good. I feel a new energy and disconnect the interior appliances from the main cable, which I slip out through the porthole at the front of the *roef*. However, I forget that there is nothing holding it to the barge on the other side, so when I go out on deck I find my electricity cable has disappeared. It is, in fact, hanging socket end down in the water. This is not good.

I expect to see blue flashes lighting up the harbour, but there is nothing at all – just a sad looking piece of moulded plastic floating a few centimetres beneath the surface. Fortunately it is still connected at the mains, so it hasn't sunk without trace; I can retrieve it, but of course the power has tripped out. To make things worse, I don't have a key to the central switch box. This is double trouble, as it seems that my second offering to the water gods is not going to be a private affair.

I sigh wearily and set off to confess all to my landlord.

Rotterdam is famous for its wind, and the Nieuwe Maas River acts as a very effective funnel. The gales mostly come in from the west and are squeezed upstream with intensified force. These are the times when cycling, my principle mode of transport, can be extremely hard work – especially if you happen to be going in the wrong direction, which somehow, it always is. It often amuses me to see the tenacious cloggies biking along the riverside boulevard in these winds. If they are heading east, the wind takes hold and simply pushes them along with great gusto. Pedalling is thus virtually unnecessary and other tasks can be performed with casual nonchalance at the same time, such as making phone calls or sending text messages. In fact no effort is required at all and it is, quite literally, a breeze. On the other hand watching the cyclists coming in the other, westerly, direction is like witnessing a tortuous endurance test. These brave souls are struggling with every pedal push; their hair is forced back from the roots and flattened against their skulls; expressions of pain and suffering can be seen etched on their faces. The contrast is hilarious.

I have been staying at my daughter's flat on the south side of the city while I prepare the Hoop for occupation, but now I am busily transferring my odds and ends by bike across the river, like an ant on wheels. The wind is giving me problems though; I have to fight to keep upright. My gallant steed is heaped up with an assortment of bedding, clothing and household goods, but the last trip over the Willemsbrug finds me blown away, and my possessions and I tumble together into the road. Somewhat unnerved but otherwise unhurt, I scramble to collect my things together, climb back on my bike and wobble unsteadily towards the Hoop, and safety.

Tonight I am at last sleeping on board and I must say I am very glad to be indoors, snugly protected from the onslaught outside. The barge rocks in the gale, and I enjoy the sensation of being on the water. I have filled my oil stove, and I've left the empty fuel cans on deck in my eagerness to be warm. Remembering them momentarily, I vow to put them away safely, but then of course I forget.

Tucked up in my box bed, which is only just long enough for even my very average-for-an-English woman length, I can hear the water slurping and lapping against the hull. It sounds as if it is in the barge with me, and my tired imagination toys with the possibility of leaks and, consequently, sinking ships; but not for long. Within minutes, I am fast asleep.

The next morning I wake shivering with a cold that chills me to the bone and I am stiff and miserable with the damp. The Dutch call this *waterkoud,* which fits the feeling perfectly. My stove has blown out, but I don't realise this immediately, as I think it has run out of diesel again.

Pulling jerseys and gloves on with numb fingers, I stagger out on deck to find a depleted stock of jerry cans, and am reminded of what I forgot last night. It seems that at least one of them has upped and 'gone with the wind'. I have also lost my *puts*, a bucket with a long rope used for deck washing, and a broom. On the plus side, the wind has dropped, so maybe the water gods are appeased. They should be. They have now had a wealth of offerings from me alone, but I feel certain that these won't be the last.

I am reminded of an incident the previous year when I was first in the harbour with my erstwhile husband. There was a violent storm – in fact, my first close encounter with the unleashed furies of the wind in Rotterdam – after which a whole plethora of random objects could be seen bobbing about on the choppy surface of the water. Walking along the Haringvliet where I now live on the Hoop, I was looking out for a chair that had taken a dive from the deck of the Kaapse Draai, when I met Andrew, a neighbour who lived on a pretty barge partly noted for its typical phone-box style wheelhouse. He was peering into the water as he walked, and his face wore an expression of both anxiety and perplexity. He glanced at me briefly, and went back to his study of the murky depths.

"Have you seen my wheelhouse roof?" he asked, his voice hopeful. I shook my head, apologising. Apparently, the said roof hadn't been secured very firmly and, in one particularly powerful gust, the whole thing had launched itself into the air and flown gracefully off into the distance. Andrew had chased after it, but his last sighting was when it had apparently gathered speed and height to clear the bridge at the end of his section of the harbour. He confessed sadly that yelling at it to come back hadn't helped in the slightest and that he feared it had gone to join all the other 'wind falls' at the bottom of the harbour.

I have since been told that the river bed is littered with an assortment of bicycles, chairs, tools and mobile phones, all sacrificial and unexpected offerings to the great Gods of the Waterways. I start to muse on all those unheard voicemail messages that must be down there. I wonder too if the message alert tones do anything to upset marine life sonar signals, or do the fish gather round and make obeisance to these strangely noisy 'creatures' that have arrived in their midst

CHAPTER THREE
Village People

Living among the 'boat people', as I jokingly refer to them, is something very special and rare. Certainly here in Rotterdam I am experiencing more kindness and generosity than almost anywhere I have ever lived, barring perhaps the equally precious folk I shared my life with on a farm in rural South Africa.

But I am learning that the Oude Haven and its neighbouring harbours is much like a village cloistered in the heart of a large city. Everyone seems to be willing to help without any expectation of a return favour, and this is refreshing for me. Coming from the cut-throat society of Johannesburg where each favour granted is noted in some hypothetical score book, and the phrase 'you owe me' is learnt at mother's knee, this unsolicited kindness is sometimes bewildering. If these 'village' folk have things that are extra, they simply give them away. Even if they are as poor as church mice themselves – and many of them are – they look for no payment or exchange trade.

The background to our floating village is as special as its people. The Oude Haven is the oldest harbour in Rotterdam and also the first museum harbour in the Netherlands. The idea for designating its use exclusively to historic boats was first conceived in 1978 by a group of owners with the help and support of the Rotterdam city council.

At that time, the centre of Rotterdam was still undergoing its own resurrection, following its virtual obliteration in 1940. Unlike the Phoenix of legend, however, it was not re-erected in its previous likeness, for at its inception as a museum harbour, the Oude Haven was surrounded by building sites from which emerged the famous cube apartment blocks as well as other modern flats. Below these, though, are colourful cafés, bars and restaurants which, with their lively terraces, form a vivid backdrop for the collection of ageing craft rocking gently at their moorings. In fact, only the 'Witte Huis' – once the tallest office block in Europe – and a short row of gracious, terraced houses stoically remain to remind us of Rotterdam's pre-war character.

To its west is the Wijnhaven (wine harbour), an extension of the Oude Haven, which is also home to a number of historic barges, and is another part of our village. Among the boats moored here are two special barges used as workshops by professional restorers, whose skills include pretty much everything from the traditional technique of riveting to the hand-crafting of lee-boards.

To the east lies the Haringvliet, another 'suburb' of the Oude Haven, a mainly residential off-shoot in which there is a more varied collection of craft ranging from classic yachts to fishing cutters. Although most of these are lived on, some are businesses such as charter ships and even offices. In a nutshell, these harbours effectively make up three distinct quarters of a unique kind of settlement.

Like most conventional, land based communities, social contact in the village is principally with the folk in your own neighbourhood, but although the Hoop is moored in the Haringvliet, I have spent time with harbour dwellers from all three quarters. I suppose that being the foreigner certainly gives me more curiosity value, and also saves me from the scourge of most villages – partisanship – so my friendships cross the barriers of the harbour's bridges.

Mireille and her head-banging, heavy metal husband live on a former Amstel brewery barge which, with its unadorned hold and flat profile, is reminiscent of an aircraft carrier. They are living in the Oude Haven proper while they do some major reconstruction. There is another identical former Amstel barge in the Wijnhaven owned by two young classical musicians, who have built a sound proof studio in their hold where they can practise their viola da gambas without interruption from the sounds of angle grinding, needle scaling and welding which are the constant back drop to life in these environs.

In short, there are young families with babies and toddlers, artists doing the alternative lifestyle thing and older couples who have come to the barging life in retirement and who want to go travelling without leaving home. Finally, there are others like me who simply love that certain something about living on the water with all the peace and tranquillity that seems to come with it.

Early pioneers of the Oude Haven's special Foundation tell me that its purpose was to create a suitable environment for owners dedicated to restoring their old boats to their original or authentic form. But here lies the rub. Who is to say what is authentic? Indeed, nearly all barges went through some form of development after they were built, even in their early years.

For example, most 19th century sailing barges had engines installed in the early 20th century, as did horse-drawn canal barges. In others, living accommodation, which was at first confined to the *roef* (the aft cabin), sometimes had extra accommodation built up behind, in front, or even on top of it to provide more living space. Then some barges that originally had open steering positions had the luxurious addition of a wheelhouse when the skipper could afford it. You could of course argue that all of these practical improvements were authentic and shouldn't need to be removed. After all, no one would consider tearing down the 15th century wing of a 13th century house, would they?

Anyway, the story goes that to help the confused and undecided barge owners resolve this thorny problem of authenticity, the Foundation set up a commission of wise and knowledgeable experts to examine each boat accepted into the harbour. To this day, the commission studies every owner's restoration plan and gives advice on what is (or isn't) acceptable in terms of the harbour's standards, and although the personnel have changed over the years the evaluation process remains the same. It goes something like this:

Firstly, an appointment is made with the applicant barge owner, who is always anxious at the prospect of these rather serious events. Then, at the stated time, two or three earnest individuals turn up and scramble in and out of every nook and cranny on said owner's precious hulk of rusting steel. Heads are scratched, deliberations are made and a report, giving recommendations on the restoration of the barge, is then written with which the owner *must* comply – which of course he or she vows most enthusiastically to do.

The criteria seem a bit vague to me, but then I'm no expert and sometimes it really is difficult to decide on what yardstick to use in a particular barge's evolution. There is one definite condition, though. The hull of the barge must be at least fifty years old and unmodified. Other than that, the feeling is that the boat's silhouette should be restored to either its original form or one that it had while still in active service as a cargo-carrying vessel fifty years ago. In other words, no fancy modern structures on the hold, cabin or wheelhouse, and absolutely *no* windows in the hull.

On the other hand, if the barge now has a modern engine, the owner is not obliged to replace it with a monument – although some of the keener types do. What's more, as nearly all the boats in the harbour are used for live-aboard, it is generally accepted that windows discreetly placed between the hatch boards or steel cap of the hold are admissible, but like so many things in Holland this is not officially allowed, it is simply tolerated. There are, however, a few purists who are so devoted to their historic principles they forego even this concession to modern life.

The slipway and workshop area, the Koningspoort, is probably unique for a museum harbour. If it isn't, it is almost certainly the most comprehensive in the Netherlands, and the facilities are booked up for at least a year in advance. Run with business-like efficiency and wry good humour by Bert, a former engineer, there is rarely a day when the slipway is not occupied, but woe betide the owners who dare to forget or cancel their booking. Such a transgression is about the only thing to put Bert in a bad humour, as he is justly proud of his 'good attendance' record.

Apart from this, there are fully equipped wood and metal workshops, which are available to all the harbour dwellers to help them with their restoration projects. There is also a shower and toilet for use by those who haven't yet built their own on board; an amenity I am immensely grateful for. Waiting my turn for the shower is a great chance to socialise with my neighbours. Clutching our towels and wash bags, we can exchange chit chat, pick each other's brains about technical problems, or even put the world to rights – if the shower's current occupant is having an especially long scrub.

The vessels represented in the 'museum' are a wonderful testament to the trading history and wealth of the Netherlands. The Oude Haven itself contains quite a mixed bag of craft, as it is the principal restoration area. Among them there are several *klippers* and *tjalks*. Most of these are finished or near-finished projects, and retain their place here by virtue of the fact they are sailing craft. The scene changes week by week, though, as boats come and go and, of course, there is often a visiting barge awaiting its spell on the slipway.

The Wijnhaven is mainly designated for the larger motor barges and, apart from the two work ships, there are several large Luxe motors.

The Haringvliet is a sort of 'fall-out' area, in that most of the barges there are no longer eligible for the other two harbours, because they are no longer authentic. In short, their owners have made modifications that do not comply with the Commission's requirements, so they can't be part of the museum section. Nevertheless, many of boat people prefer to be moored there as it has more in the way of mod cons. On its south side there are convenient floating jetties, against which the boats are fixed, meaning that the rise and fall of the tide is not an issue in terms of whether you go up or down the plank to your boat. They also have the luxury of cable TV connections and much smarter showers and toilets, installed mostly for the benefit of visiting cruisers. On the downside, the mooring fees are quite a bit higher, so there is a real price to pay for these advantages.

The Hoop is moored on the north quay, which is effectively the 'wrong' side of the street, but I prefer its position. Where the others have the conveniences, I have the sun – a rather better bargain to my mind.

On reflection, life in our community has many parallels with the rural village – everyone knows one another; news travels through the community faster than an SMS and everyone shares each other's joys and tragedies in equal measure. The only real difference between our rural counterparts and us is that here, all the 'villagers' have one interest in common – the barges on which they live.

Any conversation with a neighbour is likely to end up in a discussion on the same old subjects – what they're doing with their barges, what progress they've made or how they're going to solve a particular restoration problem. To take it further, any visit to or from a neighbour will inevitably result in a study of recent changes and developments. Such open scrutiny would be considered rude by the average house dweller, but such is the passion for their *schip* that the bargees would be seriously disappointed if their friends did not actively remark on their latest improvements – even if only to say how they would have done it differently.

That being said, everyone is careful not to live in each other's pockets and privacy is well guarded. Even so, there is a vibrant community spirit prevailing, and there's always help at hand when it's needed. Fairly typical of the average rural community, you might say, but what is not so typical is the fact that this is right in the heart of an inner urban area in one of the most densely populated regions in the world. It is indeed a rare and special place, and I am learning its ways with increasing pleasure

CHAPTER FOUR
Learning Curves

Pigs might fly.

There are always days when things just don't go right, when you know you should really have submitted to fate and stayed in bed, but to have weeks like this simply isn't fair.

Most of the time I'm very happy with my new life, and find the novelty and pleasure of being a water gypsy brings new experiences to enjoy every day.

I love just sitting in the doorway of my wheelhouse with a cup of coffee and watching the ducks, for instance. They live their own life in their own world, and it's endlessly fascinating to watch their busy, bossy interaction with each other.

I also revel in the simple tasks of sweeping my decks and washing them clean. The knack of throwing the *puts* upside down into the harbour and then pulling quickly on the rope, so that it acts as a scoop and emerges full of water, is a skill I have just learnt. It's ridiculously satisfying, and it feels wholesome and honest – a task that has been occupying skippers and crewmen for centuries. I even like taking my containers and fetching water from the taps on the slipway. The sight of me staggering back to the Hoop, much like a beast of burden with my load, is probably quite amusing as well.

But there are downsides to this life, mainly the result of my inexperience, and this current run of ill luck has made its mark by virtue of its annoying length.

In brief, no matter how many words I've had with the Boss, nothing has been going my way for an entire week now. All in all, I've been on the Hoop for just over a month and this particular episode started last Friday morning when, after a night of driving rain, I woke to find I once again had no power. My oil stove hasn't worked since the last gale blew it out, and for some reason I haven't been able to get it going at all. As a result, I've been relying on an electric fan heater.

No power, then, meant disaster on more than one front. I was cold (as usual), I couldn't make coffee, and there was no way to heat water for a wash – each a catastrophe in its own right. What's more, I had to go to work and with the February mornings still being very dark, I couldn't see to dress. At this point, I concluded that the fates were against me, so I decided to give myself up to them for half an hour or so and phoned work to say I was sick – not adding of course that my sickness was of being frozen, caffeine free and late. Then I went back to bed to consider my fate. At least I could better deal with the cold snuggled up in my duvet.

Warmth has a way of revitalising the grey matter, and so, deciding I had to sort my power problem out to effect a cure for my ailments, I sought out my favourite landlord as soon as I had mustered the courage to get up, and asked him for the keys to the mains box – again. I could only assume that my current system was not tough enough to withstand the effects of below zero temperatures, and that it had just tripped out under pressure.

When I found him, he was wearing a welding mask, so only his teeth flashed a greeting. Then, seeing my face and crumpled demeanour, he pushed back his mask and solicitously asked what had occurred to make me so very frazzled at such an early hour. After hearing my sorry tale, he offered to lend me his car the following day to go and buy a decent cable. In other words, one that was both waterproof and freeze proof. I accepted gratefully, and the teeth gleamed again. In the meantime, he gave me the key to un-trip the switch and fix a temporary repair, so as to move onto something constructive and mood improving. This was to be my 'doggy plank' project.

Only a couple of days before, my ex-husband had asked me if I could look after the dogs while he was away on business, and they've been with me since. One of them is a black Labrador called Daisy, and the other is Polly the Collie. They came with me from South Africa when I flew here but, given the confines of my current accommodation, they've stayed on the Kaapse Draai. Understandably I've missed them so I've been very happy to have them for a while. Being rather elderly ladies, however, they find it difficult to negotiate the rather steep stairs into my tiny *roef*, so the task of helping a heavy old lab and an arthritic sheep dog up and down these dozen or so steps has proved to be something of a challenge.

Daisy stands at the top and waves a hopeful paw at me, her dear face all wrinkled up with worry. We then go through a ritual performance of me clucking and encouraging until she plucks up enough courage to launch herself into my arms and we both tumble onto the floor with me providing the soft landing that she wants. An encore is then performed with Polly who can only come down on three legs anyway, because the fourth is a bit useless. She tends to just let go and cascade down the stairs in a flurry of tail and paws. After a couple of days of this, though, I thought I could alleviate the problem for all of us by making a kind of internal *loopplank* or gangplank.

So, after I'd made my first coffee of the day and fed and walked the dogs, I collected a plank of chipboard from the hold and proceeded to saw short lengths of 2 x 2 to act as footholds. Creating this masterpiece took me the best part of the morning, and by the time I'd finished I was pleasantly warm as well.

Pleased as punch with the final product, I took it inside and put it in place. Tails waving with mild interest, the dogs stood and watched me from the wheelhouse, where they have taken up residence for their daytime lounging. They find it easier to get on and off the ship from here too, which gives it an added attraction. So, once the new model stairway was fixed in position, I suggested to my canine friends that they might find this new arrangement more to their liking. I was wrong. The two dogs took one look at it, then looked at each other with an expression that clearly said "too risky!" and "Blimey, who does she think we are?" and proceeded to slither down the gap at the side. What a failure.

To make matters worse, that evening the Spanish omelette I had made on a small gas ring as comfort food ended up on the floor when the pan just slid gracefully off the flames. Supper score: dogs two, me nil. I resorted to toast and peanut butter.

To continue with my diabolical week, Monday brought my opportunity to search for a decent, strong cable and taking off in Phil's car, I found what I thought I needed at a store some distance away. Success achieved, I congratulated myself and, after arming it with the necessary accoutrements, I tried to fit it.

Failure. The shop had given me the wrong connectors and, to add insult to injury, Philip told me I should have bought one twice as long.

"At least as long as the ship," he said. "But don't worry, I'll get you one." He smiled engagingly.

Yes, Philip, I thought. And that will be when squadrons of little pink porkies fly formation over the Oude Haven.

On Tuesday I borrowed his ancient red Golf again. This time it was to look for a fridge.

Failure. Despite the February cold, there is apparently a fridge shortage in Rotterdam. Every *kringloopwinkel* or second hand shop I tried claimed to have had a 'run' on *koelkasten*. The sales people all shook their heads and clucked sympathetically, but sorry, they said, trying out their unaccustomed and rather formal English, "no refrigerators".

"I'll get you one," said Philip on my return, and the teeth winked at me in the afternoon sunlight. I thought of my elusive shower and toilet. Where *are* those pigs when you need them? I almost got excited the same evening when he called to tell that he actually had a fridge for me. He just needed to measure it. Several days have passed since then and nothing even remotely resembling so much as a cooler box has appeared in this vicinity.

I have now lapsed back into my normal state of suspended anticipation and have set up a nightly vigil for sightings of those elusive porkies. I have now accepted that this is just my week of constant failures, which sometimes happens when you live on a barge. I keep reminding myself that it's part of the adventure, especially when I consider the owner of this one and his unique relationship with flying animals of a peculiarly pink and porcine nature.

In fairness, though, Philip came this morning and fixed my stove, which is now providing tropical conditions within. At the same time he put a hand rail on my stairs, which of course the dogs will find very useful, and gave me a beautiful old mirror to hang over the fireplace; the result of this is that all illusions of having an exotic and youthful reflection as usually seen in shop windows have now been cruelly shattered. However, I only need to sort out that nagging problem of a decent cable and fridge, speaking of which I still don't have, and hopefully my adventures in electricity will be over for good.

There are still a few other problems to put right. One of them is the leaky diesel pipe, which is the result of a spontaneous act of thoughtfulness by my landlord. There is a two hundred and fifty litre fuel tank in the engine room, which he has had filled for my heating needs. Like most such acts, however, he has forgotten another equally spontaneous decision which was to saw through the copper pipe that fed the engine in order to make a connection directly to my stove – a plan which has never reached completion.

This morning, after thanking him profusely, I went below to inspect my wealth of fuel only to find both the sawn-off pipe and the tap dripping rapidly into the bilges. After alerting Philip to the literal pouring away of all that money, I watched him stuff plugs into the offending orifices, while listening with interest to his very vocal expletives bouncing off the surrounding steel walls. Given that I need to use the tap to decant fuel for my heater, I am rather perplexed now about how to get at it so, although my stove is working hard enough to heat the Albert Hall, this might be a short-lived pleasure.

The other problems are minor compared to the prospect of another chill setting in, but they are still there. In other words, I still have no running water, no washing facilities and the toilet is still sitting upside down in the wheelhouse. I use a camping loo which has to be emptied once a day, meaning another trip to the office on the slipway, and my dirty clothes are loaded into big bags and taken to the harbour laundry room, where there are coin operated washing machines.

Life seems to be rather basic and a far cry from the centrally heated warmth of my former homes. Nevertheless, although sometimes hard work, it is never boring, it is nearly always entertaining, and I wouldn't change a single thing.

Advice can be nice.

The weather has turned bright, crisp and icy cold. Going outside is like opening the door of a deep freeze, but it is so clear and sunny, I have decided to start giving the wheelhouse a face-lift. When I moved onto the Hoop it seemed that the doors were in most need of attention; they hung in cracked frames and broken hinges, and showed signs of coming apart at every joint. Although nothing has changed I have shelved this idea for the moment, for one very potent reason. Every time I make a conscious decision to repair the broken sections and hinges, it snows. This has happened so many times now that I've decided to wait until such a likelihood becomes an impossibility. The doors will be fixed in the summer.

Instead, prompted by the cheering prospect of a day of sunshine, I am busy stripping off the old varnish and am delighted to see the beauty of the old teak emerging. There is nothing quite like working with wood to restore one's equilibrium, and I know that when it is finished, it will glow with warmth and depth. I can hardly wait.

However, one of the drawbacks of the kindly community of self-made experts in the harbour is that everyone has their own ideas about how things should be done – and they are all different. Consequently, I am receiving a steady stream of advisors on board who, with a knowing shake of a shaggy head, or the scratching of a stubbly chin, will give you their own version of 'the only way' to achieve perfection – based on personal experience of course.

Standing out on deck doing this kind of job is rather like lighting a fire in the bush. Every creature – in this case, harbour dweller – is drawn to your ship through an irresistible curiosity. They tend to stand on the quay and watch through half closed eyes, making thoughtful sucking and chewing noises as if they are physically working on what they are about to say.

Bearing in mind it is now early March, I am slightly peeved that the first advice I receive is that I should have done this job before the beginning of winter to provide the wood with the protection it needs against the rigours of the harsh weather. This statement is of course made with complete disregard for the fact that I wasn't even here then. The next 'advisor' tells me that in fact the best time to do it is in August, and that I should wait until then; that it's pointless to start now. I do not retort that if

I wait for even another couple of months the whole structure is liable to collapse completely, probably with me under it. In the end I do what wisdom dictates – nod, smile, agree, and then carry on doing it my own way.

I enjoy these casual visits, though. The interest is genuine and you can often pick up some very useful tips. One neighbour has told me how I could even out the colour of the teak by using something called *ontweringswater* – loosely translated as 'unweathering water'. I don't know what's in it, except that it is slightly corrosive, but it has a remarkable way of making the wood look almost new again and removing the stubborn grey patches caused by too much exposure to the elements and too little care and attention.

Another has shown me how much more effective it is to dilute the varnish with turps for the first few coats, as this helps it to soak into the grain of the wood and improves its protective layers. In fact, only the final and sixth coat should come straight from the tin.

These practical tips have all been valuable, and I especially like the way in which they are delivered as, after the bravado of the criticism, the really useful advice often comes out rather shyly and is only tempted forth by a cup of coffee and a cookie.

Then, of course, Mireille the Oracle comes quite often, settling herself and her tummy into my tiny living space and giving me all the guidance I need on where to find the right tools and what they are called in Dutch.

Every day brings added knowledge and new experience. I realise that I am still very much a novice at this life, and that being a 'stranger in a strange land' adds to the challenge, but when it comes to woodwork, I feel at home. It is something I can connect with, and taps into a fund of normally well-disguised patience. Even the willing helpers are allowed to have something to offer, though the main message is not always what I want to hear. That apart, there is always more to learn and, for a project such as this, I am happy to be the eager student.

Gradually, then, the wheelhouse is emerging from its state of pitiful neglect to be a thing of unique beauty. It is widely recognised as being special because of its age and elegant design, and many of the barge owners seem pleased that I am doing this job. The Hoop's presence in the harbour pre-dates the inception of the foundation for these historic barges and is therefore regarded by many as the 'queen' of the Oude Haven, enjoying a special status and affection. I can imagine that her gradual slide into decrepitude was watched with sadness by most, and that now there is some care being lavished on her, the resurrection is being watch with equal approval.

I probably won't finish the wheelhouse before the spring, but at least it is now clean and stripped of all the flaking varnish, moss and mould. I will have to spend several hours sanding it down and then filling in holes and cracks before applying even a single coat of varnish, and all this will have to be done when the weather permits. I don't mind, though. Indeed, I rather like the fact it will keep me busy for some time to come. There is plenty more I can learn in the process – maybe not about the work itself, but certainly about my watery neighbours.

CHAPTER FIVE
March Madness

The Little Sister

Today, I have a new friend, of the four-footed variety, on board. Well, to call her a friend may be somewhat premature at this stage, but she is certainly an entertaining, if somewhat nerve-wracking addition to my small furry troupe.

She has come to me via Philip's bright and cheerful girlfriend, Angelique, who stopped me on the quay the other day and suggested I might like to have a kitten. Seeing that such a desire hadn't been high on my list of priorities, I was somewhat taken aback, until she explained the situation.

Apparently the kitten used to belong to Philip's daughter, who is now pregnant and doesn't want to combine cats and cradles. It seems she is afraid of disease. As I know this is something that alarms many young women when they are pregnant, I wasn't all that surprised. Still, I told Angelique I would need some time to consider. After all, another animal means another tie and, while I am only too happy to have the dogs, a cat creates its own restrictions in that you cannot take it with you whenever you go away. Dogs are infinitely more transportable. You know: have dog, will travel, but have cat and you're bound to the flat – or the house – or, in my case, the boat.

Nevertheless what Angelique started, Philip has finished, because yesterday morning he arrived clutching a small thing under his arm that bore a greater resemblance to a flick-knife-wielding, hissing cobra than to a cat. In fact, all I could see was a small mouth opened in a perpetual hiss and two rigid front legs with every claw fully extended, ready to inflict maximum damage.

"Val", my landlord coaxed, with that inimitable smile, "Angelique tells me you're willing to take little *zusje* off my hands." Seeing my obvious hesitation, he pressed home his advantage: "I'm so grateful, and I know you'll take good care of her. I'd keep her myself, except that she doesn't like my own cat, and now he's upset, so…"

What could I say to such a charm offensive? I've always loved cats; I've always had them too, and at one time when I myself was pregnant, seven of them slept in a heap on my bed, taking turns at being in the centre of the mound.

So now I have Sisha, so named because I didn't realise that *zusje* means 'little sister', and immediately anglicised her name to what I, in my ignorance, thought Phil had called her. Sisha is small, lithe and tabby all over, and having her with me seems to be much like having a naughty two year old on board. On the other hand, she is an adorable, affectionate, purring, head-butting bundle of love – wrapped up in a skin of complete and utter mischief.

The first thing she did on being deposited inside was to examine every nook and cranny of the Hoop's diminutive living area. This exploration entailed climbing behind the backboards of the cupboard below the sink in my miniscule kitchen and then howling indignantly because she couldn't find the way out again.

I had to clear out the entire contents and remove all the shelves just to make enough space to get myself into a position that was sufficiently contorted to be able to haul her out. At first, the dogs greeted her arrival with much nervous tail wagging and some agitated shuffling in their beds as if they knew she was about to usurp their places. However, they watched the rescue with smug interest, and Daisy tried to help – or hinder – matters along by nudging my backside every now and then, which in turn made me bump my head against the back of the cupboard. Naturally, I cursed each time she did this, which inevitably startled Sisha who, of course, backed her way even further into the recesses of the Hoop's hull.

Eventually, though, I managed to grab her by the scruff and pull her through, spitting and clawing until she realised she had been rescued. The transformation was instant, and I then became her heroine as she purred furiously and wrapped her small sinuous self around my legs in a delighted little dance. As she cruised, she made enthusiastic 'puddings' on the floor to further demonstrate her pleasure at being freed.

This morning, however, her adventures are taking her out into the big wide world. She knows the harbour already, so I can't keep her in. The only thing I am worried about is that she will go back 'home' again to Philip's barge, but I doubt it. She didn't like the feline competition she found there in the first place.

As I sit in the wheelhouse with the dogs, trying to do some preparation for work, I realise I am spending more time watching the 'child' prance along the top of the hold, chasing leaves and pouncing on imaginary 'kills'. Everything looks all right so far, so I resolutely go back to my reading, but then I notice Polly pricking up her ears as she sits in the open doorway.

Looking up, I freeze in horror. Sisha is no longer on the hold. She has decided to tempt fate by 'tightrope walking' along the rim of the hull, the *potdeksel* in Dutch. Unfortunately, fate has the upper hand today because the predictable happens and she slips and falls with a splosh and an angry wail into the harbour. The crying is instant and deafening and I rush along the side to see where she is. What I see is awful: my soggy little kitten is desperately trying to claw her way up the harbour wall!

Obviously she can't do it but, not lacking determination, she turns and, like a tiny grey seal, swims the length of the barge, trying to find some way of climbing out and crying pitifully all the time. Panicked, I chase after her and attempt to hang the only thing I have of any length over the side of the barge: a scarf.

I try waving it at her, in front of her and over her, which she, of course, ignores. What I think I can achieve with this I don't really know, but at least it seems like *something*. Maybe she will have a flash of super-human intelligence and realise I want her to cling on to it so I can pull her out. But then, maybe I am being optimistic about the likelihood of such enlightenment under these circumstances. After all, Sisha is a cat in water. Not generally a good combination at the best of times, and if she were that intelligent she wouldn't be swallowing water and wailing like a banshee right now anyway.

Nevertheless, I must look even more pathetic than the cat to Phil who, hearing the din, rushes over from the neighbouring barge where he is working. Without a second's thought he climbs over the side and, while hanging on to one of the mooring ropes, scoops up my bedraggled and soggy moggy and hands her to me with a terse comment to get her dry. Suitably cowed and humiliated, I do as I'm told.

Sisha is none the worse for her experience though and as I dry her she allows the dogs to snuffle her damp fur. Despite the fact that she looks for all the world like a long legged rat, she resumes her purring and head butting as if nothing worse has happened to her than a brief burst of rain

It seems that the dunking hasn't taught Sisha much, and this isn't the end of my feline nursery problems. I keep her indoors for a few days in the hopes that she will forget her dance of death along the edge of the barge, but this is a new week, so I decide to let her out again and see what happens. She springs from the deck to the hold. So far, so good. Then she springs straight from the hold to the *potdeksel* again. My heart stops. She wobbles a moment, rocking to and fro, with all four paws clinging to the rounded lip. It is a truly breath taking moment, but then she finds her balance and trots off confidently. This time, though, she goes right up to the bows and jumps neatly over the metre wide gap to the barge in front where Phil is doing some welding.

Cursing not so quietly, and sweating with anxiety, I run round and head her back home. The last thing I need is a cat with arc-eye after a close encounter with a welding torch. By the time I am back on board the Hoop again, however, she has disappeared again. This time the contents of my stomach threaten to stage their own exit, and everything else sinks to my boots. What am I going to do? The two dogs, with their dear, sympathetic expressions, watch me with concern written all over their faces. They don't know whether to retreat to a quiet corner or give me comfort. I feel bad that this small, troublesome minx is taking so much of my attention from them. It doesn't seem fair when they are so patient.

I spend the next hour pacing round the harbour, asking everyone and anyone if they've seen a small tabby cat. Passers-by are accosted, and look at me curiously when I say falteringly, "*Hebt u mijn* tabby *poes gezien?*" I don't know the Dutch word for 'tabby', so hope they know mine. The looks are clearly puzzled, so perhaps not.

What can I say to Philip and Angelique if I've lost her this time? Almost in tears, I go home to collect my thoughts. She can't have gone far, it's just not possible, so I turn off the radio and sit and listen. Then I call her, but the dogs get excited and think I'm calling them, so I have to settle them down again and we all sit and listen.

Eventually, I hear a single, plaintiff cry, which seems to be coming from one of my clothes cupboards. I look inside, but there is no sign of Sisha. Calling again, I hear another cry. It is definitely there, but I still can't see her, so I take out all the clothes and then I spot it – a small gap below one of the shelves at the back and, sure enough, I can see a movement behind it.

Somehow or other, in the short space of time it took me to return from the neighbouring barge to the Hoop, Sisha managed to climb into my cupboard (the door of which refuses to close) and find a hole to crawl through. But, as is invariably happening with this cat in this barge, she cannot get out again. Maybe not so surprising, though, as it does seem to be true that cats can't go into reverse.

The problem now is how to extract her from her self-imposed internment. I try coaxing her with pieces of food, but since all I have access to is her rear end, this doesn't prove to be very effective. I try clutching at the only thing I can reach with a couple of fingers, but find I am just pinching her tail, which merely serves to annoy her and make her hiss at me. In the end, I realise there is nothing for it. I will just have to take the whole cupboard apart.

It takes me an hour to unscrew the shelves and dismantle the interior of the cupboard, vowing to myself that if she ever does this again she can jolly well stay there. As I free the first of the back boards Sisha leaps cleanly out, shakes herself off and promptly walks over to Daisy's basket, where she settles down to wash herself clean of the cobwebs and fluff she has gathered.

My poor dog looks at me helplessly. Something in her expression says very plainly, "See, Mum, I knew that was going to happen all along. I knew she was going to take my bed. And now she has!" And she lies down with a heavy, resigned sigh and puts her chin between her paws. It's a dog's life when there's a cat involved, isn't it?

Over the next few days Sisha establishes herself as queen of her realm. She is by turns passionately affectionate and insufferably superior. The poor dogs are bossed around without mercy, although in truth she seems to like them and is quite happy to share their beds with them; a move that neither Daisy nor Polly is altogether sure about.

She also secures her position with the other neighbourhood cats, and the flick-knife claws are frequently put to use in her struggles to gain another inch of territory. I sometimes hear these skirmishes when I am lying in bed, as it sounds as if I have the feline equivalent of an Errol Flynn action scene taking place over the hold.

The skittering paws and angry howls are punctuated in my imagination by feats of astonishing 'derring do', but in fact, Sisha and her adversary are just rolling each other head over heels as they are locked in a furious clinch. She doesn't appear to come to any harm though.

I am becoming blasé about her ability to spring from barge to barge regardless of the size of the gap between the boats, and her normal route invariably has her prancing along the *potdeksel* as if she is continuously and deliberately trying to flout fate.

Not since the cat I once had on a farm in South Africa have I encountered such a character in a furry suit. Sisha is exasperating, *eigenwijs* (wilful), temperamental and loving. She hates to be picked up and cuddled but loves to sit on my lap, head butting me and rubbing her face over mine. She cannot bear being kept in, and howls with outrage when I close the doors and windows over night to prevent her terrorising the district. In truth, I have the feeling she is only semi domesticated at best, and wonder how long she will choose to stay with me. For now, though, the little *zusje* is keeping all of us on our toes.

What the wind blows in

Apart from trouble in a cat suit, March brings me another new friend. The evening in question is cold, dark and blustery and I'm sitting in the Hoop's little salon listening to the radio, feeling slightly sorry for myself. The dogs are snuggled up in their beds, snoring gently; Sisha is out on the prowl somewhere, and I'm alone. I feel that very strongly.

I try reading but my mind wanders; I am too self absorbed, I know. Suddenly I hear a knock, or what I think is a knock. I look at the dogs, but they don't react. Not all that surprising as they are both a bit deaf. Puzzled, I climb up the steep steps and push the hatch open into the wheelhouse. Looking out, it is inky and the street lamps only offer limited pools of light around their bases, but I think I can see a movement. It is the swirl of a long black coat. Then I see a familiar stride, which belongs to a tall, lanky figure that seems distinctly recognizable.

I open the door and call, "Koos? Is that you?"

The coat swings again as the figure turns and, emerging from the darkness, the street lamps reveal that it is indeed Koos.

I met this Dutch answer to an English gentleman last year when he was working on his own barge project in the harbour. He was frequently kind to me when I was out of sorts with life, even though he was experiencing some personal character building challenges himself at the time. In the course of those few months we developed a friendship of sorts, and it was with him that I had my first real taste of water travel.

Shortly before I set off back to Johannesburg Koos had announced that he would be taking his *dekschuit*, or pontoon barge, back to Leiden, where he lived, and invited me along for the ride as far as Delft, where I could jump ship and catch a train home very easily.

The Saturday of the trip dawned grey and blustery with the guarantee of rain but nothing daunted, I joined Koos and his son, Sanne, on board the Luxor in the Oude Haven. There was no shelter on his barge, as its steering position was open, and he'd only just built the steel box over the original deck in which he was going to create his home. It was merely a shell, so provided no comfort away from the weather other than a solitary chair which Sanne quickly occupied, settling himself down to read. He promptly went off to sleep, as young people do, and spent the whole trip thus ensconced, oblivious to the lack of comfort.

Predictably, the heavens opened almost as soon as we were too far to turn back, and for the fourteen or so odd kilometres to Delft I held an incongruously bright green and white-striped umbrella over Koos as he stoically steered his Luxor through the driving rain. Needless to say, we were both soaked through by the time we arrived at a good mooring place in Delft, but I'd had so much fun with this particular skipper and his quirky sense of humour that it was altogether bearable. After warming up with soup and coffee at a *gezellig* (cosy and intimate) café, I took the train back to Rotterdam with a smile, squelchy shoes and some good memories.

Consequently, I am rather pleased to see him now, as he is bound to have brought his good humour with him and I could do with some of that.

Koos has an air that reminds me of top hats, capes and gas lamps. He would have fitted perfectly in the Edwardian London of the early twentieth century, as there is something distinctly old world about his charm and his rather elegant turn of phrase. Add to this a dark brown velvet voice with a permanently wry twist and you have a character with a capital C. He speaks almost perfect English, professes to speak German even better, and French very competently. In Holland they call this 'having the language knob', and I am wistfully envious as I have more of a language 'block' myself.

Luckily, I have two *stoelen* (seats) these days, although one of them is just a folding deck chair. Koos lowers his length into it, and I make coffee while I ask him why he is here. I cannot imagine he has come all the way from Leiden on this foul night just to see me, and I am right. He has interrupted his journey on the way back from Lille, where he has been attending a meeting for the next *Voile Lille* to celebrate the '*Journées du Patrimoine*', which will take place in September.

It seems that every year since 1996, Koos has organised for a fleet of historic Dutch barges to sail to the Bois-Blancs, a particularly impoverished area of Lille, as part of festivities designed to nurture a sense of culture and community in the area. The local people have found a permanent place in Koos's heart, and he tells me how much he enjoys seeing the pleasure on their faces as they line the quays to watch the barges enter the harbour.

"They all know me, Val, and they value the effort we make so much. It's worth it just to see the joy they feel when the procession of boats comes through the open bridge. And, of course, I love being star of the show." He grins at me, and for some inexplicable reason I believe him, despite the twinkle in his eye.

With my decorative oil lamps casting their soft glow over my simple abode, we sip our coffee and chat with the ease of good companions. He tells me that he is bringing the Luxor back to Rotterdam some time next month, and will more than likely be staying permanently, as he has applied for a *ligplaats* (mooring) here. Koos's marriage, like mine, has hit the self-destruct button, so we have some common ground to share. Given the circumstances, we both feel this calls for a drink – whether to celebrate or commiserate is not quite clear –

but the problem is that I have nothing in stock, so we decide to go to the local watering hole, which is conveniently close to the Hoop.

Entering the Weimar Café is like walking into a meeting of all the harbour's residents, for almost everyone is there. Philip and Angelique, Joram and Karin, the musicians, Frits, a sculptor turned barge restorer and his girlfriend José, and a dozen or so others that I know by sight but not by name. They all know Koos, of course. And they see us together, of course. And they all jump to conclusions, of course, which surprises us both.

It turns out to be a good evening. We all drink just a little too much, which results in cheerfulness of an unrestrained nature, and the bonhomie flows as freely as the wine and beer. At some point Koos decides it is time to catch his train home, and so we leave together, deliberately ignoring the over-exaggerated winks of our friends, who have now forgotten discretion in the fog of inebriation. It is all well meant though, and is unlikely to be remembered tomorrow.

At the station we hug our farewells, and I once more go home with a smile and some good memories after spending several hours in the company of this gentle man.

Above: Traditional barges all in a row
Below: A beautiful sailing clipper

Harbour 'liggers' removing an old engine for overhaul

CHAPTER SIX
Spring Fever

The air is spiced with a fresh tang and a hint of spring, which has brought a flurry of activity to life. A week has passed since Koos's visit, and I have been able to settle into life on board and take stock of things that need to be done with renewed enthusiasm. These are numerous and, in some cases, urgent.

Some jobs need doing regularly on any boat, and it is rather like doing external housework. The decks have to be washed down at least once a week, the *roef* needs to be scrubbed and the canvas tarpaulin covering the hold needs to be kept free of dust, leaves and, ultimately, moss.

On the Hoop these routine chores hadn't been done for a very, very long time before I moved on board. There are thus large areas that I haven't managed to attack yet, which consequently still look sadly dirty and neglected – a fact which prompts one passer-by to inform me, "You can wash your decks as well, you know!" as I am throwing out the dish water.

Somewhat mortified, I know he is right, and that these tasks should be chalked up as urgent.

Also urgent is the cleaning and painting of my tiny 'loo' and kitchen, or at least the areas that serve as such, plus the re-tiling of the fire place in the salon. The tiles themselves are stacked up on the floor in the recess behind the *kachel* (oil stove) gathering dust, fluff and grease from the diesel that drips from a slightly leaky feed pipe. They need to be attached to the wall behind the stove with big brass screws and washers in traditional barge style, and these I will need go in search of. The kitchen is already tiled in the same fashion but the screws are black and grimy with age, so I will have to take each one off and clean it separately. It is a practical system, though, because with the movement of a boat tiles stuck with glue or other adhesives could well fall off and break after a period of time, but those that are screwed on will hold under any conditions.

I also need to fix myself up with some more electric lighting, as reading by paraffin lamps at night is not doing much good to my already myopic tendencies. So many things to do, but what should be done first?

I decide on the course of least mental resistance and with a *puts* and brush, I scrub the top of the *roef* behind the wheelhouse. This makes such a radical difference it even raises an eyebrow and a word of praise from Philip. Thus encouraged, I then scrub the canvas tarpaulin, ridding it of its film of green moss, and finally wash off the decks again. With the wheelhouse stripped of its ancient and flaking varnish, and an altogether cleaner ship, we are starting to look almost decent, and even some of the other *liggers* (harbour dwellers) not only look on with approval but even comment kindly. This makes me feel good.

A period of cold, grey and wet weather then ensues and my outdoor spring cleaning is curtailed. I start to focus on the indoor tasks, but cannot help feeling depressed that it doesn't take long for all my exterior labours to be almost totally reversed. In this climate, with this level of urban pollution, I realise how often these simple maintenance jobs will need to be done, and I pause for a moment to play with the image of a householder rushing out to scrub his brick walls and tiled roof every week. It is an entertaining thought, even though it serves to highlight how much more work is involved in living on a barge.

One brief high spot in this period of uninviting chores is my first attempt at throwing ropes. The Rival, the neighbouring barge, has been in the Oude Haven for a week or so, having some work done at the *werk plaats* – the special area that is designated for noisy structural jobs. Today, it arrives back just as I reach home after a morning's teaching.

I have just changed when I hear a commotion, and I look out of the wheelhouse in time to see the Rival being nudged alongside me in readiness to pull it into its berth. Calling out to Frits, who is standing in the bows of the slowly moving barge, I ask if I can help and, to my surprise and consternation, he says yes. I swallow hard. I am not very practised at this rope business and it can be quite tricky unless you know what you are doing. I, of course, don't, but as they say, 'nothing ventured'.

Roping a barge into position when it is being towed or pushed by a smaller boat is a matter of attaching the ropes to certain strategic posts, or to other barges, in a way that takes account of the movement of wind and water. For example, if you are entering a mooring with bows to the wall, or 'car park style' as I call it, you have to take a rope which is fastened at the stern of the barge and walk at least half way towards the bows with the looped end in your hand. As your vessel is being nudged into place you must be ready to throw the looped end over the post at the rear of the berth (or on a neighbouring boat), so that the barge can be pulled the rest of the way in. Then someone standing in the bows should throw a line to someone else who is hopefully standing on the quay to attach it to the mooring poles on the shore. Alternatively, they can sling a rope onto the foredeck bollards of a neighbouring barge, if there is one.

By this time, if there is any kind of current in the harbour, your barge has probably swung out of line at the stern end and will need to be hauled back in to lie neatly alongside the next barge or at least 'parked straight' in its mooring. This involves leaning back with your rope tightly in hand and bracing yourself against the hull as you pull with all your strength – depending on your size, of course. The whole procedure may sound simple but, suffice to say, it can be mystifying and quite difficult for a former landlubber like myself.

In any event, Frits asks me now to throw the looped end of a rope over a very tall post just ahead of the Hoop's bows so that he too can pull the barge forwards into place.

I fear I will never do it. Playing cowboys with lassoes was never one of my childhood skills. With three brawny men around me, though, I have to try – and then, much to my delight and astonishment, I fling the heavy gnarled rope over the post at my second attempt.

Undiscovered talents. I smile to myself and crow inwardly with delight, despite the fact that the three brawny men in question take it all totally for granted.

Life is full of surprises here in the harbour, and the most unexpected for me is that I have now changed my mooring, although I'm not sure yet that this is a good thing.

One of the benefits of living on a barge is that you can move your home whenever you wish but, by the same token, your home can also *be* moved. By others. Whether you like it or not.

It happened a week or so ago, just after my triumph with the rope. The weather warmed up quite suddenly, so the tour boats resumed their regular trips through the harbours. It seems that they wanted somewhere to disgorge their passengers in the Haringvliet and so they approached the Haven Museum to negotiate a convenient spot. Unluckily for me the 'perfect place' happened to be where I was lying with the Hoop, and so the bustling little Director of the museum told me that I had to be moved. Not the next day, not the next week, but right then. Was that OK with me?

Hmm, I considered, better talk to Philip. Which he did – right then.

A short time later a powerful tugboat pulled up alongside and Philip jumped aboard, smiling his big smile and announcing that we were going to be towed to the Oude Haven as soon as the Bridge Keeper had arrived to open the way for us.

It so happened too that Mo, my daughter, had arrived from South Africa for a holiday the day before, so at the moment we were about to be unceremoniously removed from our comfortable berth in the Haringvliet, she was still in bed. Still, she must have become aware that her world was on the move, because she struggled up the stairs into the wheelhouse with her face all squashed up with sleep and her hair still mussed by the pillows.

We were already coupled up alongside the beefy tugboat belonging to a friend of Philip's and, to Mo's confused mind, it must have looked as if we were about to be towed out to sea.

"Where are we going, Ma?" She questioned me anxiously. She hadn't been counting on an ocean cruise.

"Not far, pet. It seems we are surplus to requirement in this spot and we have to relocate! Orders of the big boss," I said with a smile, although I wasn't best pleased about it.

At that moment I noticed something that neither Philip nor his tugboating friend had seen. We were being pulled slowly away from the quay, but we were still attached to one of the mooring poles on the harbour wall by a long, but forgotten, rope.

I charged out of the wheelhouse and started up the *gangboord* (gunwale), yelling frantically to Phil as I ran. As I caught his attention I pointed to the rope, which was beginning to be pulled taut. If we didn't get it off in time it would snap under the strain, and the whiplash effect could cause some serious damage to any object in its path – or, even worse, to an unsuspecting passer-by.

I have never seen anyone move as fast as my usually laid back and amiable landlord. The teeth gleamed again, but this time in a grimace of sheer horror as he leapt over onto the Hoop and bounded up the barge in full panic mode. Rapidly releasing the rope from the bollard on the starboard side, he flicked it off the pole on the quay with an ease that must have been generated by a potent mixture of fear and adrenalin. The subsequent grin confirmed that we were clear of danger, but I was convinced this near disaster could have been avoided and my face must have said as much. His expression began to look slightly sheepish, but the agreement was tacit.

Weak with relief, we head off to our new 'address' at the north end of the Oude Haven but, instead of being moored with one side to the wall, we are now being presented with a new challenge. The Hoop has to face the quay in 'car park' position, which means the *loopplank* must be hooked over the prow of the barge with its base on the quay. The gradient at both high and low water is much steeper. With no handrail, a novice of a daughter, and two elderly dogs to help on and off, life is certainly becoming increasingly interesting.

My place in the Oude Haven is very different from my former mooring. For a start, it seems to be darker as I am more enclosed, both by other barges and by the buildings and trees. It will take some getting used to. It is also much noisier as I am surrounded by cafés and bars, most of which stay open till the early hours of the morning at weekends. Then of course Thursday night is Student Night, when the local hostelries offer special discounts for the young and highly educated. Add to this *highly spirited* and *highly inebriated*, and the volume increases tenfold.

Mo helps me manage the dogs for the short time she is with me, so that they get used to being manhandled onto the *loopplank*. For Polly, who is still light and relatively dainty of foot, it is not a problem once she is perched at the top. She just skitters down and lands neatly on the pavement. Daisy, however, is more of a handful, but mainly because she's nervous. Probably aware that her greater size and weight are a disadvantage, she seems to grow roots into the top rungs of the *loopplank*'s cross bars and has to be pushed gently but very firmly from the rear before her paws can be prised from their terrified grip. Then, all at once, she breaks free and dashes down in a tumble of clumsy legs, arriving on terra firma quite safely and wagging her tail in pride that she has done it – again.

Sisha is, of course, unperturbed. She is already ruler of her entire world, so she is just happy that there are further corners of her realm to be explored, including more boats with endless nooks and crannies to be investigated.

I am a little further from everything, though. The walk to the shower is longer, the distance for carrying the water containers seems much greater, and for a while I mourn my old spot, as I can no longer sit in my wheelhouse doorway with a clear view of the waterway in both directions. On the plus side there are even more ducks here, and it is quite a nursery as there are several mums with their tiny families zooming round between the boats, peeping excitedly. They nest in the rowing boats that many *liggers* have tied up beside their barges and it is quite enchanting to see the babies hurrying after their mothers, learning how to dash for the crumbs of bread we throw them.

The harbour sounds are different too. In the Haringvliet I went to sleep with the regular slapping of the river against the hull, as the water is constantly flowing through the bridge there and the current is quite strong. At this far corner of the Oude Haven, however, there is little such movement; it is very shallow and, at low tide, the Hoop settles on the bottom. The oxygen escapes in bubbles from under the barge, so there is a constant 'glub... glub' sound as they burst on the surface – quite unnerving at first, as it can seem as if the boat is sinking.

One of the other things I miss is the boat traffic. There are a couple of party boats moored opposite my former spot and they make regular trips out of the harbour, so it was quite common for me to hear the roar and thrust of an engine going into reverse, and the thrashing of the propeller as the boats manoeuvred themselves out of their berths. I don't have that kind of activity here and it feels like a loss.

Added to that, I no longer see the neighbours I have become accustomed to: Frits and José, who were just round the corner and could always be relied on for some good cheer, even if it was just a wave in passing. Then there are Simon and Marietta, who were my 'back end' neighbours. Their sturdy old motor *tjalk* is very well suited to Simon, who is also solidly built and wears his slightly wistful smile like an amiable bear deprived of his honey. Marietta, on the other hand, is slim, kindly and practical, and seems to have kept an eye on me over the past few months.

On the way to the shower this morning I am pleased to see her, and we stop to chat for a moment. It is, as usual, a disjointed conversation as her English is limited and my Dutch is worse, but we do manage to communicate somehow. She sees my towel and clucks with disapproval that my long awaited washing facilities have still not materialised.

"Wil je een bad nemen?" (would you like a bath?) she asks. I stop, mouth dropping in wonder. A bath? An actual bath? How long is it since I've been able to

immerse myself in a full tub of piping hot water? The idea alone sends shivers of ecstasy down my spine.

"Heb je een echte bad, Marietta?" (Have you got a *real* bath?) I can only just breathe the question.

"Natuurlijk!"(of course!) She almost scoffs, as if she, unlike me, considers it a perfectly normal thing to have on board. *"Kom je vanavond."* (Come this evening.)

I return to the Hoop unshowered and tell Mo my news. She is going back to South Africa and to as many baths as she likes in a few days, so her amusement at my reaction to this event is tinged with pity. The point is that baths are not really the norm in the Netherlands at all, and it is only relatively recently that new houses and apartments have been built with full bathrooms. For the most part the older flats, and even the larger homes, only have showers at best.

That evening I head over to the Haringvliet with a rucksack full of luxurious soap, towels and wonderfully decadent smelly things. Marietta gives me a tour of their barge before leaving me to my wallowing. Their living space is huge compared to mine, and it is bright with primary colours. Like its owners, the whole atmosphere is very homely. They have two small children, which is evident by the scattered toys around the living room. The bathroom she leads me to is as large as that in any house, and I notice with pleasure that the soap dish is home to a collection of plastic ducks and boats to make the evening soak more enjoyable.

I run the water, climb in and indulge in the most wonderful feeling ever; that of being totally submerged from chin to toe in delicious, scented, bubbly water. The sensation is heady, so that when I climb out twenty minutes or so later I am definitely feeling slightly woozy.

Relaxed and languorous, I thank Marietta profusely but refuse offers of coffee as I just want to prolong the after effects and climb into bed, totally warmed through and squeaky clean.

Climbing up their steep steps and out through the hatch, the cold night air hits me and I suppose I must already be slightly giddy from the warmth of my bath, as the next thing I know is that I have lost my balance and I am keeling over the side of the barge.

The iciness of the water is shocking as I plunge to its depths and I flounder, astonished and bemused that I have ended up down here at all. All sorts of absurd thoughts flash through my mind, such as that my towel will get wet – obviously a disaster; or that I mustn't lose my rucksack, which is of course securely on my back and is the last thing I am likely to part company with.

I manage to surface before the need to gasp for breath overwhelms me, and I immediately start looking for a place to climb out. I can swim perfectly well but I am rather over burdened with clothes and bags to do much more than flail about, and besides, it's freezing in here!

A voice calls out to me from above.

"Val, are you there?" It is Marietta, calling to me in English, and her voice is brimming with laughter – although she does sound a little worried as well.

"I'm okay," I call to her, "but how can I get out of here?"

She directs me to the end of the barge where a rope ladder hangs down, ready for just such an eventuality. Pulling myself up, the water streams off me and I must weigh twice as much again with my saturated clothing. Marietta helps me out, laughing with relief that I am unhurt.

"Wasn't one bath enough for you?" she jokes.

"Well, I thought I'd make it Turkish style," I quip, and we both collapse in hysterical giggles. I have twigs hanging out of my hair, my leather jacket is dripping and sodden, and my mobile phone, which was in my pocket, decides that this is all too much and dies in my hands. Nevertheless I am still in possession of my rucksack, although the contents no longer bear any resemblance to things of a luxurious nature. This apart, I am fine but shivering with cold again.

Marietta offers me another bath, but I decline. Now I really do want to go home and get warm. I also want to share the tale with Mo, as I know she will double up with laughter.

As I trudge round the harbour, past the bars and cafés, I watch people watching me with half embarrassed interest, and I chuckle to myself. I must look a comical sight. The twigs are still adorning my hair, my shoes are squelching and I am leaving a trail of puddles behind me as I walk. I feel quite certain that this is an incident I won't be able to keep quiet and that, although I have defied the water gods in a rather undignified manner, the story will have assumed much greater proportions by the time it has been round the harbour a couple of times tomorrow.

Spring and Koos make their entrance to the harbour simultaneously.

Walking up to fetch my post from the office, my spirits lift as I feel the softness of the air on my face. The buds are breaking out and the birds are positively shouting their pleasure in the year's re-birth. It suddenly makes me feel very optimistic.

Looking into the harbour, I notice that Koos's *dekschuit*, the Luxor, has arrived. I didn't see it come in, but suppose it must have been while I was away teaching. Of the man himself there is no sign, and then I recall that he is also bringing his little tugboat, the Loeki, so that he will have somewhere to live while he busies himself preparing the Luxor as his home – perhaps he is on his way.

The post box reveals nothing of interest, and I head round to the small bridge house where the washing machines are housed. With a load transferred to the dryer and another pen stroke next to my name on the list of harbour residents using these machines – a simple but effective accounting method – I lock the door and turn to see the bridge keeper preparing to close the gates, so as to lift the section of road for a vessel to pass through.

This is a sight I always love, and I have wasted many minutes leaning on these railings to watch the passage of a barge or two. It just so happens that this time I know the skipper, as the boat in question is indeed the Loeki with Koos at the wheel. What a pretty, graceful boat it is! Painted a shade somewhere between cream and yellow, it has long lean lines and looks spectacular on the water.

Koos slows down to turn the corner after the bridge and, with the consummate ease of a true master, he manoeuvres his tugboat deftly into place next to the Luxor. It all looks so easy, but I know for sure that there are few people who have that intuitive feeling for the wind, currents and behaviour of a craft that Koos has. Maybe he can teach me a thing or two about steering?

That seems like a good thought to play with and, with this pleasant plan in mind, I retrace my steps round the harbour to welcome the newcomer in.

CHAPTER SEVEN
Changes And Developments

The warmer weather has brought everyone out of hiding and it is such a pleasure to see hatches opening up, *liggers* sitting out on deck, and everyone with smiles on their faces. It makes me think of moles emerging from their underground world. Walking round the harbour can now take some time as there are so many people busy with exterior maintenance on their barges that I have to stop several times to pass the time of day with my neighbours and admire the work in progress. It often seems to me that you have to have a passion for paint to live on a barge and that every year this particular love affair has to be renewed with vigour.

For myself, I am particularly thrilled because at last I no longer have to carry containers to the yard to fetch water. I can open a tap in my kitchen and have as much as I want – well, up to a thousand litres in any event.

The installation of this glorious luxury was not without drama, and was conducted with what I now see as my landlord's inimitable gift: a combination of improvisation, near disaster, and the help of the long suffering angel that watches over him.

Philip arrived last Saturday with a flat pack containing what looked like a large folded black bin bag, and an impressive roll of polyurethane pipe. When he informed me that the bin bag was in fact a one thousand litre water tank, I thought he was pulling my leg. Nevertheless he disappeared down into the hold, so I followed him to see what he was going to do.

I'd noticed a grand old machine towards the far end of the hold that was wreathed in cobwebs. I'd assumed it was an oversized air compressor, but Philip now told me that this was the *hydrofoor* (water pump) which keeps the water inside a large seventy five litre flask at high pressure to ensure that it pumps through in a constant flow to wherever it is directed – in this case to the kitchen and, of course, the bathroom. If and when that day eventually comes.

While explaining how it worked he unfolded the flat pack, and I was impressed to see that it was indeed very big. Spread out on the floor, it looked like a plastic sheet of about two square metres but, he told me, when full of water it would look like a massive black pillow. Apparently, bags such as these are often used in boats where the only available space to place a water tank is of an unusual shape. These flexible containers can mould themselves into the shape of the designated area, which makes them quite versatile. I think the reason for putting one in the Hoop was just because it was easy to carry on board and install – or at least so Philip thought.

The next trick was to fix the inlet and outlet pipes. This job proved to be more difficult than anticipated. The tank's flexibility was in fact a drawback when trying to keep the pipes in place while Philip tried to tighten jubilee clips around the joints. The slippery material refused to comply and repeatedly escaped from the handful of thumbs Philip seemed to have developed. As the air started to crackle with expletives, I beat a judicious retreat and went off to make coffee.

When I arrived back in the hold with a steaming mug and a plate of biscuits, Philip flashed his habitual smile to assure me that all was well again. He'd moved on to Stage Two, which involved attaching the main pipe to the *hydrofoor* and rolling it out along the floor of the hold. As there was nothing else in there except wood and building materials he'd decided there was no need to channel it along a special duct, so it just meandered across the floor. I had my doubts about the wisdom of this. Supposing someone trod on it and burst it. Supposing Philip himself crushed it with the things he stored in the hold. The images ran riot in my mind, but I kept them to myself.

Stage Three was feeding the pipe through the engine room and then through the floor behind the sink in the kitchen above, so that it could be attached to a tap. First, though, he had to drill a hole in the sink for the tap to sit in. I imagine this was another case of things seeming to be much easier when you are just planning them. What he hadn't taken into account was that the sink is very old, and made of a kind of Italian marble. It is actually lovely, with its mosaic style basin, but definitely not designed for twenty-first century fittings.

Drilling the required orifice was therefore not a 'just' job, and took as much time as it did for me to wisely disappear again and go off to the market to do my shopping. A Philip without a smile was too sombre a sight for me, and while the stone chips mingled with the sparks from both his drill and his mouth, I felt it prudent to keep my distance.

On my return, equilibrium had again been restored and he informed me cheerfully that he was ready to test the system. The tank had been filled, and if I would now please stay in the kitchen while he turned on the *hydrofoor*, I could then turn the tap on to check for leaks.

As it happened I didn't need to check anything, as the moment the water started pumping through, a jet stream of positively painful force squirted out from under the sink and caught me full in the face. What my friend had failed to mention was that the hot tap should remain firmly closed, as the pipe from the *hydrofoor* was only attached to the cold water inlet. The other inlet for the hot water feed had no connection to anything and was left open ended. Unfortunately for me, the hot tap itself was already in the open position and so the water just took the line of least resistance and made for the nearest exit – the free inlet pipe. My face just happened to be in the way of its rush for freedom.

I ran to the open hatch and screamed at Philip to turn it off. He peered up at me with a look of wide-eyed dismay, but by the time he'd heard me most of my living area was soaked. After grimly mopping up and hanging rugs, towels and cushions out to dry, I learnt the reason for the spraying I'd had and we came to the conclusion that, ironically, the soggy outcome of the test meant the system did actually work. Nevertheless, we agreed we should still check it again to make sure all the joints were leak proof, something my high-pressure face wash had prevented me from seeing.

The second attempt was a more scientific affair and revealed that one or two of the brass fittings needed tightening, to which Philip duly attended, but when I asked what he planned to do about the hot water inlet he just grinned and told me to keep it in mind.

"You'll have hot water soon, don't worry," he soothed. Somewhere overhead I caught a fleeting glimpse of some small, pink, cloven-hoofed animals flying circles around me. But then it was gone.

Sighing in resignation, I resolved to put a cup or something similar over the tap so that I wouldn't be tempted to turn it on by accident – which luckily I haven't, so far.

The plus side is that life has suddenly become a whole lot easier, and every day I fill my kettle and pots with conscious appreciation. It is amazing how thankful one can be for a convenience the rest of the western world takes for granted. After four months of fetching my daily rations in two ten litre containers, I have biceps to die for, but am cheerfully ready to return to flab if it means the daily joy of watching a steady flow from a chrome-plated outlet in my own home.

The *hydrofoor* has been quite an experience, though. Because it is so large it takes quite some time before I use enough water to trigger the pressure switch that starts it pumping from the tank into the holding flask. As a result, I woke up in alarm in the middle of last night when I heard a terrible grinding, grating noise. It went on for about a minute and then stopped as suddenly as it started.

This morning I realised what it was. I got up during the night to get a glass of water, and this last half-litre or so that I drew was the trigger that set the pump off – but only after I'd climbed back into bed and gone to sleep again. It's a terrible noise, and sounds as if there's a monster growling and gnashing its teeth in the depths of the hold, so I'm very glad it doesn't do it too often.

Nevertheless, I am so happy with this relative luxury, I don't care at all whether the equipment is state-of-the-art modern or lifted from Noah's ark. I am just certain I will never be complacent about the worth of what it provides.

Another development that has taken place is the completion of my wheelhouse project. The bright, dry weather we have been having recently has given me the opportunity to spend the lengthening evenings sanding, smoothing and varnishing the stripped teak until it now glows with a warmth that gleams richly in the late afternoon sunlight.

I am inordinately pleased with the way it has turned out as I have cherished more care and attention on this part of the Hoop than on anywhere else.

Also completed is the re-painting of my 'bedroom' which I have finished in a soft white with all the panelling in a glossy deep crimson. The wooden floor boards of the salon are the same rich colour, which is typical of traditional barge décor, while my cupboard sized kitchen is trimmed in blue and yellow. In addition, all the tiles behind the sink and cooker have been individually washed and every brass screw has been removed, polished and replaced in the centre of each one. They positively wink at me when they catch the light.

I have also been busy with the white tiles behind the stove in the salon. Luckily, most of them already had screw holes in them, but some of them hadn't been pre-drilled so, at the cost of a few breakages, I have learnt how to make the holes needed by using a drill bit made especially for ceramics and applying the pressure very carefully so as not to force the process. The *kachel* now looks very smart with its clean, shiny back panel, punctuated by the brass screw heads, and I have applied special black polish to the stove itself to give that a face lift as well.

With all these interior jobs done, I can spend more time outside in the fresh air and focus on refreshing all the paintwork on show.

As the days pass and the evenings become ever longer, I live increasingly on deck, where I am periodically joined by one or other *ligger*. I am glad of this since the dogs have now gone back to my ex-husband, Mo has returned to South Africa, and Sisha spends more time swashbuckling her way round the harbour than she does at home.

My most frequent visitors are Mireille, whose practical level-headed outlook on life is a foil to my rather wilder enthusiasms. She makes me laugh, but she also keeps my feet on the ground. Her calls are mostly made in the afternoons when I am home from teaching assignments and we drink coffee and share biscuits on the foredeck out of the sun.

In the evenings, Koos has become a regular as we have taken to sharing meals together on the 'cooking for two is cheaper and easier than cooking for one' basis. We are also finding we share more than just food, and spend hours chatting about work, travelling, ideas for barges and so on, but most of all about music.

On one recent occasion, we were sitting on the *roef* and I was extolling the delights of living in such extremely compact accommodation.

"I love it," I enthused to Koos. "Everything is me-sized."

With a smile of a rather different nature to the one I was used to, he responded.

"That's good, because I rather like 'me'."

I think of this somewhat minimal exchange quite frequently these days and realise that this is a development that might well endure, if allowed to stand the test of time.

Progress is being made in my hopes to become competent at steering a boat myself. Having never attempted anything more challenging than rowing a dinghy when I was a child, the idea of 'skippering' my own barge has so far been something of a pipe dream. Now, though, I am eagerly awaiting the call to make loose the ropes that tie the Loeki to the land because Koos, his son Sanne and I are taking a trip upstream from Rotterdam. The destination is the harbour at Vianen and the purpose is to join a tugboat convention, which is taking place there this weekend.

The day is dazzlingly bright and deliciously hot, a perfect Saturday; there is practically no wind, and the occasional piece of fluff that passes for a cloud looks incongruous and unreal against the clear blue backdrop of the sky.

There always seem to be so many preparations to make before casting off, but in fact it's not so complicated, just time consuming. Being moored long term in the harbour means using the shore facilities so, when leaving, these have to be disconnected. The electricity cable has to be unplugged and untangled from all the others it has somehow become entwined with. Even worse, those of us who have fixed telephones on board have to unravel metres upon metres of phone flex because the connection points always seem to be disproportionately far away from the barges. To prevent them trailing in the water, we have to loop our cables one over another on hooks sticking out from the harbour wall – a recipe for endless knots of frustration.

After our grand scale version of 'cat's cradle' with power and phone lines, we have to sort out the ropes. These can also be something of a confusion as, over the weeks, barges and boats come and go, so that the last in has their ropes within the easiest reach. If you don't move for some time, they can get quite 'bedded down' and be rather difficult to untie. Fortunately, Koos hasn't been here very long and his are easy to extract, so finally we are ready to go.

I am glad Sanne is here too as I don't know too much about manoeuvring, and although I offer to help, I'm not too upset when Koos assures me with some solemnity that it won't be necessary for me to protect the Loeki from any chance knocks as he doesn't intend to hit anything. I have the feeling he just might be teasing me.

With the powerful Gardner engine thrumming beneath our feet, Koos eases the tugboat from its mooring and, performing the boating equivalent of a three point turn, we head towards the bridge. The bridge keeper has already been called and I can just imagine him pedalling furiously up the Haringvliet from his post at the Boerengatbrug, at the other end. Sure enough, he appears now as he swings himself off his bicycle and moves to close the barriers across the road, ushering stray walkers, cyclists and last minute cars through before the red and white gates block the way.

Slowly the entire section of the road lifts. Koos, who has been holding the Loeki steady just before the opening, puts the powerful engine into forward gear and we slip smoothly through. Passing between the ranks of moored barges, other *liggers* call out and wave and I feel ridiculously happy to be here, on this day, on a boat going 'faring' as I call it. I've had to resurrect this old English word in an attempt to express in my own language the Dutch word *varen*, which is their verb for travelling on the water. In fact, the inland waterways are called the *binnenvaart*. I know that our own rather romantic 'farewell' for 'goodbye' originates from the German word *faren* (meaning to travel), which is of course where the Dutch *varen* also comes from. As the only other options in modern English for describing this form of travel are 'boating', 'sailing' or 'cruising', none of which feels right for what we are doing, I have come up with 'faring' as a more apt description. And so we fare away, out of the harbours and onto the Nieuwe Maas, heading upstream.

There is a light breeze blowing and the river is busy with both commercial and leisure traffic. Being a Saturday, there are powerboats galore and in places, even water skiing. Along the banks there are several small beaches and these are crowded with cheerful Dutch families, all well stripped and oiled and taking in as much sun as they can absorb on this unexpectedly glorious day. We pass through the outskirts of Rotterdam, and the landscape beyond is typically Dutch – in other words, unrelieved by so much as a molehill. Nevertheless, with the trees fully dressed in their spring greenery, the countryside looks rich in its pastoral, flourishing lushness.

About ten kilometres out, we reach a fork in the river. To the right is the Noord, which leads to the town of Dordrecht, but we keep going straight on, although the waterway now becomes the Lek. With the way clear ahead, Koos asks me if I'd like to try my hand at steering. This is the moment I've been waiting for, and I am both excited and nervous.

The wheel feels huge, and I have to get the feeling of how far it turns before there is any noticeable difference in direction. It seems to pull to the starboard (right) a little, so I keep having to correct it so as to stay on track. There are buoys of varying combinations of colours and stripes dotted up and down each side of the river, and Koos explains that they all have different meanings, which I know I will never remember in just one day, but it is important that I keep close to the left of the ones that mark the main channel. This impresses me, as even I don't think the huge thirteen-hundred ton barges will be very charmed if a small meandering tugboat steered by a crass beginner crosses their path.

As the Loeki ploughs on I start to relax and enjoy myself. It feels like a real holiday with the clean bite of the breeze, the penetrating heat of the May sunshine and the sparkle of the reflections on the busy waterway. I smile at the two men in my enthusiasm. They both smile back at me indulgently. They have done this many, many times before.

Eventually I relinquish the wheel to Sanne and retreat to the rear deck to enjoy the ride, exchange banter with Koos, and watch the passing scenery. Another thirty kilometres and roughly two hours on from the fork marking the start of the *Lek*, we arrive at the turning which will take us into the lock separating the main waterway from the harbour at Vianen. I have yet to find out what is needed when it comes to 'locking through', so I leave it to Koos and Sanne to find a place among the throng of other boats which have also arrived to join the event. They are nearly all tugboats, and it looks as if they are all trying to cram their way in, as it will take some time before the next crop of boats can pass through.

The difference in the level of the water between the river and reclaimed land of the *polder* on the other side is not very impressive for so big a lock. Today it is only about a metre, although Koos tells me that if the river is high then it is a different situation. The lock itself is built for barges of up to 110 metres long and 11,5 metres wide, so the Loeki, at a modest 16 x 3,30 metres feels like a rowing boat by comparison.

Once everyone is in place the massive gates close and the water level starts to drop. In no time at all it is over, and the gates at the other end open up so that the small flotilla enclosed can escape into the canal beyond.

Ropes are untied, engines revved and the procession of tugboats exits. As we emerge I see quite a sight up ahead: row upon row of tugboats moored up against the right hand bank of Vianen harbour. There is bunting, music and the sound and smell of good cheer. This is an Event with an emphatic 'E', and there are crowds of visitors thronging the towpath. Unfortunately this is where I will take my leave, as I have only come along for the ride and now have to find a bus that will take me into the nearby city of Utrecht, where I can catch a train back to Rotterdam.

Sanne is also leaving, so once everything is made fast Koos joins us in our walk to the bus stop, a path that is frequently interrupted to greet and meet his old acquaintances. I can't help noticing how these weathered skippers all look at me curiously as if they are bursting to find out who I am. Then one of them finds he cannot restrain himself.

"And are you Mrs Koos?" he asks daringly.

"No, *meneer*, I'm just me," I respond, with a smile to Koos himself. His answering grin is full of understanding. There is nothing wrong with his memory either, it seems.

Minutes later, Sanne and I are climbing aboard the bus to take us back to Utrecht. The journey home seems unutterably dull after the enchantment of the earlier hours on the water, and I am aware that another hook has been cast and the bait has found its target. What a wonderful way to spend one's time – and one's life. I think I could very easily get used to this.

CHAPTER EIGHT
Branching Out

Spring has merged almost imperceptibly with summer, or what passes for summer in any event. It is gloriously hot, and as a result it is suffocating inside the Hoop, which is completely uninsulated. To relieve the oven-like conditions within, I have been opening not only all the portholes but also the *koekoeks*, which are old fashioned, removable skylights. On many barges, these are very beautifully crafted from teak wood and glass, and the Hoop's are no exception. I have two in the *roef*, in fact: one large one with a rounded top whose windows are fixed, so I have to lift the entire frame off its opening, and the other with two small windows that are hinged onto a traditional pitched-roof style frame. These can just be lifted to provide an essential escape route for the heat.

Sisha now spends most of her days hunting in the bushes surrounding the small grassy triangle across the road, and I barely ever see her. She is becoming increasingly feral, and makes a good impression of playing at being a big game cat, even though she is only the size of a well-developed rat. Koos, on the other hand, joins me with noticeably more frequency and we have started making plans for further trips. Sadly, he has now sold the Loeki and is living on the Luxor, which is much more spacious and altogether more sensible for someone of his height, but I can't help missing the little tugboat. It had such a cheerful, friendly 'face'.

At the end of the month, there will be a trip to take part in a village festival at the tiny port of Strijen Sas, on the edge of the Hollandsh Diep, but before that we are going to Den Haag for another event to celebrate old *binnenvaart* barges. I find this idea thrilling as, after the excursion to Vianen, I can't wait to get behind the wheel again.

In the meantime there is still more maintenance to be done, and I busy myself with re-painting the top of the *roef,* which probably hasn't seen a lick of paint in years. I also crawl my way around the *gangboord* which surrounds the *roef* so that I can sand down and varnish the window frames. When that's finished, I put new putty around the glass, which I then paint yellow in traditional style. It is a fairly precarious undertaking, as with one careless slip I will be over the side and into the rather dubious water below. At this end of the harbour the detritus of many a night's excess at the bars and cafés tends to collect round the barges until the tide comes in and washes it out again, but it doesn't all go and I have no desire to find out how much is left.

I am revelling in all the outdoor work, though, and never tire of trying to restore the beauty of this lovely old barge. I have also taken on another project. After seeing how the Hoop's wheelhouse has responded to some generous TLC, Philip has asked me if I would consider doing the same on his tugboat. I have agreed with alacrity and, given the long spell of fine weather we are having, it shouldn't take me long.

Another feature of the European summer I am also enjoying is the long evenings. Twenty years at the same latitude south as Cairo is north means I have long been accustomed to a less dramatic change between winter and summer daylight hours. Here in the Netherlands it remains light until 10 o'clock in the evening, and even later at the solstice, so work can carry on till the day begins to fade, well after 9 p.m.

The only drawback is that I end up going to bed too late. Koos and I routinely sit out on the *roef* to eat our evening meal as it is getting dark, and then, of course, we both want to have some kind of an evening afterwards. There is no television reception here in the harbour, so we often just listen to music, or Koos plays his guitar, and the notes hang sweetly in the warm night air. It is most certainly good to be alive.

Every year in the Netherlands many of the societies for the preservation of historic cargo vessels hold events where all the gentle eccentrics with a passion for old barges can gather with their boats. The events are held in different towns to give the local people a chance to see the wonderful collection of floating monuments that still grace the Dutch waterways. This year there is one being held in nearby Den Haag (The Hague), and Koos has decided to take the Luxor along for the show.

We have made no real plans for the route we are going to take from Rotterdam, and the most direct way to Den Haag is via the Delftse Schie Canal which runs through the historic centre of Delft. However, as we chug out onto the Nieuwe Maas and head for the lock which marks the main entrance to the canal, we decide on impulse to go a bit further downstream and make a tour through Schiedam, a beautiful little town that is principally famous for making gin and having the tallest windmills in Holland. From there we know we can re-join the main canal without making too much of a detour.

Knowing that I am still a complete novice at boat handling and maneuvering, I am filled with a mixture of excitement and nervous anxiety. Luckily Koos's years of experience will probably keep me out of trouble, and so I am not too worried, but all the same the butterflies are doing rapid circuits of my stomach. The river is choppy today with a brisk wind but the sun is shining, the temperature is high and all looks good with the world – at least until we reach the lock at the entrance to the Schiedam harbours, anyway. We negotiate the lock into the town without mishap – despite my total and fumbling inability to throw a rope onto the cleats in the lock wall – and are promptly thrilled with our decision to take this route.

The lock keeper tells us we can pass under the first few bridges without difficulty, but that he will phone ahead to arrange for the next three to be opened for us. These are so low that even dinghy sailors have to duck. He also advises us to take it gently – not that we can do anything else. The canal here is lined by ancient buildings and warehouses, propping each other up like the dignified old souls that they are; then it winds its narrow way quietly through the town. Not only is it incredibly picturesque, it is also an oasis of soothing tranquility. At one bridge, a fellow bargee is there to wave us through. He has heard the throbbing of an old engine and rushes up to see what it is. For the beginning of a trip, Schiedam is a hard act to follow with its old world charm, but we are determined not to be disappointed by anything today.

Leaving the town, I take the wheel for a short spell. On the Luxor it lies horizontally, which feels strange and, added to this, for the first time I have to handle waiting for a swing bridge to open. My success at achieving this is no minor triumph, as it involves keeping the barge steady by periodically putting it first into reverse and then into forward gear again. As the one action counteracts the other, the result is a more or less immobile boat. Or should be. It reminds me of learning to drive – there are so many things you have to remember to do at once. With the added factors of wind and water to boot, I am dizzy with relief when the bridge finally opens, so to recover my equilibrium after so stress-filled an event I resort to a familiar routine and go inside to make coffee.

Within seconds of my disappearing below, the heavens open, but the first I know of it is a sharp rapping on the engine room roof from Koos – who has taken the wheel – demanding his rain mac. There is a simple equation with the Luxor in its present state: no wheelhouse equals getting wet fast. Admittedly he asked for a coat when I headed inside "just in case", but I didn't expect him to need it quite so quickly. The rain is soon over, though, and by the time we pass into the main canal the sun is already shining again.

The Delftse Schie is normally a very busy commercial waterway, carrying sand and building materials between Rotterdam and Delft, but for about six weeks in the summer the bigger of the two locks into the Nieuwe Maas is closed and the pleasure craft have the canal to themselves. This makes for very pleasant, stress-free faring and the countryside on each side of the water is pretty in a singularly Dutch way. Fat cows share fields with grazing ponies; cyclists spin along the tow paths; fishermen sit motionless in the long grass along the banks and children splash around in rubber tyres near cottages that crouch close to the water's edge. Further on, the occasional dry dock or factory reminds us of the canal's more profitable use but, although in striking contrast to the pastoral scene, they don't look ugly or incongruous. On a hot summer's day in June, the whole picture is peacefully and beautifully serene.

The Luxor's old engine belches out quite a bit of smoke, so we are occasionally greeted with pinched noses or the odd disgusted comment as a sun worshipper is enveloped in diesel fumes. Mostly, though, we are acknowledged with friendly smiles and cheerful waves as we make our way through the bridges of Delft. With another swing bridge to wait for, I am beginning to feel that maybe, just maybe, I will be able to master this maneuvering thing one day.

Delft is not very visible from the water but, like Schiedam, it is also a little gem of historic Dutch charm, and between its last bridge and its close neighbour Rijswijk there are some truly lovely old buildings lining the canal. For quite a long section there is also the tramline that runs from Delft to Den Haag, which is reputedly the longest in the country, and Koos is having great fun filming passing trams from the boat. By now too, the towpaths are growing busier and the signs of urban development more evident.

Before long we reach a point where we have to turn left for Den Haag, as to continue straight on would take us to Leiden and Amsterdam. I find it intriguing to see signposts at the water's edge in the same way that you see them on the road. Even better is seeing 'no parking' signs at places where you can't moor up. I suppose all seasoned helmsmen are used to this and think nothing of it, but it tickles me no end. Somehow I never expected to see such normal traffic directions on the water.

Having made our turn, we can now see the tall office blocks of Den Haag in the distance. We have also been joined by other historic boats heading for the same destination. In front of us is a beautifully restored *westlander*, which is a smaller type of barge than the Luxor. As close as you can get to an English narrow boat, the *westlander* was built specifically for transporting vegetables grown in the market gardening area of the Westland between Delft and the coast. They generally had open holds, which could be loaded up with goods and were only covered with hatch boards if necessary. These days they are often converted to leisure craft, but there are still some enthusiasts who maintain them in their original form, and I guess most of these will be here at this event, as there are plenty of them still around.

We are soon part of a slow procession of barges, both great and small, making a stately and impressive entrance into the harbour at Den Haag. Many of the large *luxe motors* and *tjalks* have to wait for bridges to be opened before they can pass but, with our low, sleeker lines, we rather smugly sneak through the smaller gaps and arrive way ahead of our usually faster fellows.

After trying out a couple of spots we eventually find a mooring where we feel comfortable and, with fuel and water taps turned off, we finally leave the old motor to rest. The Luxor has arrived; the engine (apart from contravening all European emissions standards) hasn't missed a beat, and we have had a wonderful day's faring. What more could we ask?

The event is like any and many other rallies of its kind – fun and colourful. This is true of all these festivals, but for me this occasion is really only a reason to enjoy one of the loveliest canals southern Holland has to offer. Arriving there merely means we can look forward to the return trip which, although the same, will be just as special. After all, we can see it all from a completely different angle, can't we?

The end of the month brings a further opportunity to free ourselves from the shore and go faring. The excuse is another event at a small town lying behind the *sas* of Strijen. *Sas* is an old Dutch word for a lock, but it is only used in place names these days as the current word is *sluis*. Many villages were built and developed around locks so, although there is a town called Strijen, the village that surrounds this particular lock is predictably called Strijen Sas. It lies on the edge of the great Hollandsh Diep but, since the dykes that protect this low lying land are quite high, there is little impression of being on the shores of a watery super-highway once the safety of the tree-lined canal is reached.

Our outward bound journey is exhilarating. As I have discovered from Koos, the best time to start faring is two hours before high water because this gives us the chance to extract ourselves from the harbour without too strong a current to hamper us. It also means we are running with the tide for a significant part of the journey, which helps us make good time, not to mention saving fuel. Today it means leaving at around ten in the morning – a very civilised hour as by this time the sun is blazing and the breeze on the river is refreshing as we emerge from the Boerengat bridge.

The Luxor's flat bottom takes the choppy waters in its stride, and even when we are passed by the massive container carriers and bulky tankers, the wash does little to disturb Koos's former pontoon barge. He has also perfected the trick of steering into the oncoming waves to reduce the rolling effect that is inevitable when a boat being driven by a modest two cylinder engine is overtaken by vast vessels with more than five times its power and speed. It's a bit like comparing a Mini to a Sherman tank. Still, we keep to the side and potter along, happy in the knowledge that we are once again 'on the way'. In this life, the 'to where' part doesn't matter – just being free from the shore is all it takes to ensure complete euphoria and silly grins of pleasure.

As with the trip to Vianen, we travel upstream on the Nieuwe Maas, but this time, when we reach the point where the Noord branches off towards Dordrecht, we go with it. The banks are lined with large warehouses, small harbours and docks. There is nothing pretty or charming about the route, but all the same it has its own appeal; and from the water, in the sunshine, everything has its own beauty.

As we approach the town of Dordrecht the signs of industry are diminishing, but then we come to the greatest crossing of all. The Noord arrives at a T-junction where it meets the Oude Maas, which itself becomes the great Merwede on its way upstream and inland. It is the busiest waterway intersection in Europe and carries most of the traffic from Europoort on its way to the Rhine. Emerging as we do from the relatively minor Noord, we can see the old waterfront of Dordrecht on the far side of this seemingly huge and intimidating crossroads. However, today we are not going to make the dash across to the safety of the town's gracious historic harbour. Instead, we are turning to the right and then, a few hundred metres further on, we will take the plunge and cross the path of the great freight barges so as to enter the Dordtse Kil – another narrower but extremely busy waterway through to the Hollandsch Diep, which is the main route to Antwerp.

The butterflies are leaping around my stomach again as we prepare to cross. In the distance I can see what looks like two monsters steaming towards us, so we will have to get a move on. I can see too that they both have their blue boards up, which suggests they are going to cross the channel themselves to head for the Noord. A blue board is the only form of visible direction indicator a barge has. It is a large, square sign, completely blue and attached to the end of a pole on the starboard side of the wheelhouse. This normally lies face down towards the deck when not in use. In principle, when it is raised to show the board, it means that the skipper wants you to pass on that side of his (or her) vessel. Normally traffic follows a 'port side to port side' system but if the skipper coming downstream needs to cross the normal traffic lanes for any reason – usually to keep to the deeper water on the inside of a curve in the river – then the blue board will be raised and the barges going upstream are required to pass on the starboard side.

In our case, we need to cross over as we have to make for the entrance to the Dordtse Kil, so it is essential that we don't impede their progress. Luckily Koos is an old hand at this type of situation and, despite the Luxor's meagre size and power, we manage to slip round first one and then the other commercial barge without incident, seamlessly joining the flow of craft going in our direction. This is the last leg of our journey, and as I look around me I see that the signs of industry are becoming more scattered and the countryside is starting to open up. It is completely flat as far as the eye can see, but with the trees in full leaf and the grasses and wild flowers flourishing, the scenery is richly green and colourful.

Once again small beaches appear on the banks, all thronging with happy splashers, and I marvel at the ability of these normally rain-soaked people to make use of every possible opportunity to enjoy their own environment. This is a nation built on a love of water. There are more boats per capita in the Netherlands than anywhere else in the world, and water sports include everything from 'skinny dipping' and paddling around in old tyres to long sailing holidays in luxury yachts. A Hollander deprived of lakes and canals would be like an Italian without pasta – unthinkable.

Finally we see the end of this stretch ahead. The glittering expanse of the Hollandsh Diep fills the horizon and I know that within another hour we will have arrived. To reach Strijen Sas we must turn to the right and skirt the edge of this wide estuary for about a kilometre, but as we move out into the open waters the old engine grumbles with the extra effort needed to make headway against the stronger winds and currents. In fact, I'm sure I hear it miss a beat and my heart follows suit. I'm not that brave a sailor and prefer the relative security of being on a river with accessible banks on either side. This is far too exposed and open for my rather timid nature.

Having an over-active and fertile imagination can be a handicap at times and I instantly see us stranded helplessly in the middle of this watery wasteland, drifting into the path of a huge tanker or container barge. Being such a blip on their radar won't help either, so if I have to swim for it I don't want to be too far from at least a buoy to perch on. Picturing myself clinging to a floating ball of stripy plastic is maybe not quite as romantic as the usual image of distressed damsels clinging to remote outcrops of storm-dashed rock but, to my mind, it is just as desperate.

Then, as if I have willed it, the engine suddenly splutters a few times and cuts out. Even though I am standing up in the bows urging the Luxor on, I spot the look of alarm skating over Koos's face quite clearly. We are so close to the lock now, I can see the big doors opening. Can we, will we be able to reach it? Koos disappears below to see if he can get us going again and I hold my breath as I watch the people at the lock watching us. I'm not sure that I can trust or believe my eyes at first, but they seem to be growing in size. Then I am certain of it. We are drifting slowly but surely towards the opening. I inhale a big gulp of air, which is probably a good thing given that a more prolonged suspension of my breathing might have had inconvenient results.

Koos reappears from the engine room and shakes his head dolefully. The old motor has had enough for the day, it seems. Anxiously we stand together as we continue to drift almost imperceptibly closer. The watchers at the lock shout to us but we can't hear them yet. They are probably wondering what we are doing but we aren't yet within shouting distance, so Koos returns to the wheelhouse to try contacting them via the VHF. By the time he comes back again we have made some progress, and indeed are almost near enough the wooden mooring posts to the right of the lock to be able to throw a rope – but not quite.

Koos suddenly brightens with the germ of an idea. He grabs his boathook, which is about four metres long and, attaching the looped end of a rope to its curved steel end, he reaches out carefully until the length of its pole crosses the gap between the barge and the first post. With a deft movement, he manages to slip the loop over a hook on the side of the post and, seeing what he has done, I quickly pick up the remaining length of rope on the deck and start to pull us gently in. We are safe at last. It is only about ten minutes since the engine cut out, but it feels like hours of horrific suspense.

Smiling to each other, we pull ourselves towards the lock and, with the numbers on the water's edge now swollen to quite a crowd, we feel both embarrassed and triumphant when they applaud our entrance to the comforting confines of Strijen's *sas*.

While the doors close and the water level drops, Koos gives the engine another try, but it still refuses to start and he glumly accepts that he will have to do some repairs while we are here for the weekend. The excitement is not over yet, though.

The lock opens to let us out into the tiny harbour beyond. However, someone on the wall decides it would be a good idea to help us out by brute force. Without warning, water begins to gush in fierce torrents into the gap behind us. The Luxor starts to rock dangerously and careers from side to side, bashing into the walls and scraping along the sides as it is sucked back into the lock by the force of water passing under and around it. In fact it is doing the opposite of what was intended and, far from being pushed out, we are held in the grip of a kind of vortex. I scream at the people on the wall, but they cannot hear me above the noise of rushing water and the Luxor continues its uncontrolled rolling from side to side as it is flung off each of the walls in turn.

Koos is also gesticulating wildly but the message doesn't get through and they double their efforts. They are clearly misinterpreting our angry yells and flailing arms for excited enthusiasm, which just goes to prove that the line between ecstatic joy and livid anger is very thin. In fact it must be quite indistinguishable, judging by the response I am getting to my furious and enraged war dance. The more I prance, curse and spit, the more they grin, laugh and open up the valves.

Luckily for the Luxor and our blood pressure, it seems they eventually get the idea that their good intentions are far from being well received and, to my great relief, the water suddenly stills. By now we are totally ragged, and it is hard to adjust to the welcome we are receiving from the other participants of the event as we push ourselves slowly out.

I am dimly conscious of the charm of the rural scene we are entering. The canal is partially covered in flowering lilies, and willow trees bend gracefully over the water. The late afternoon sun glints kindly on the surface, and dragonflies dart in erratic angular bursts in front of us as we punt slowly between the historic boats already moored alongside.

Friends and acquaintances of Koos laughingly wave us through until we find our designated spot. There are reeds at the water's edge and a tree or two to tie the ropes around. A grassy bank provides us with support for the gangplank, as well as allowing some space between us and the small houses on the other side of the street. We relax unconsciously tensed muscles, relieved to have arrived. It has been a day of mixed fortunes, ranging from sheer pleasure to sheer terror, but I suppose this is all part of the rich fabric of life on the water and the stuff of which good tales are told – in retrospect of course.

We have the weekend ahead of us to sort out the engine problem, take in some of the festivities, and maybe find time to explore some of the country. For now, we tie up, plug into the electricity connection supplied, and slump into chairs with the reviving bliss of a welcome beer.

CHAPTER NINE
Local Colour

The fine weather continues, but now the air is becoming oppressive and humid. It is difficult to find relief when it is so hot and stuffy inside, and there is little shade to be found on deck. Koos takes to working on the quay. He is sanding and preparing planks of wood to flank the steel box he has constructed to cover his living space on the Luxor. The intention is to give it the appearance of a fully loaded vessel, as this type of planking was typical of the means by which cargo was contained on a pontoon barge.

He works under the spreading branches of the trees using a pair of trestles to support the lengths he has put through the huge automated plane in the workshop on the shipyard. He has become quite a tourist attraction as he hefts the heavy boards on to his shoulder and treks up to the yard and back, providing endless photos of the genuine 'man at work' for enthusiastic tourists. Only the twinkle in his eyes gives away the fact that he is aware of the joke. Frits, Philip and some of the other *liggers* chuckle at the interest the unsuspecting day-trippers show in this apparently hard working skipper and add their own demonstrations to the show. Frits suddenly becomes very busy with a wheelbarrow, carting pieces he is working on up to the same workshop and back, while

Philip focuses all his welding activities on the foredeck of his own barge, periodically lifting the front of his mask to flash his famous teeth for the cameras.

It is actually much too hot to work very hard, and my own efforts at stripping and sanding the wheelhouse on Philip's tugboat are interspersed with the numerous coffee breaks Koos provides, as his Luxor is the next barge in the row.

Mireille is also suffering from the heat, being so close to the end of her term of pregnancy, which has indeed begun to feel like some kind of incumbency. She and her stomach have spent many a weary afternoon enthroned on my foredeck, where we sip Rooibos tea in companionable lassitude. I am on a promise to take her to the clinic when she goes into labour, so I am expecting the call any day now. Her husband doesn't drive, and gets himself around on a delivery bicycle with a huge crate fixed to the front (a *bakfiets*), but even he can see that this won't do on such an occasion. Their boat now lies in the Wijnhaven, as with the forthcoming birth they feel it will be more peaceful there than in the hub of Rotterdam's night life, the Oude Haven – but still close enough for regular visits.

On the Hoop, I have new neighbours now that there has been a summer re-shuffle. The barge lying next to me is a beautiful clipper called the *Gelderland*. It is owned by identical twin brothers, Jon and Arjen, although I have only just found out there are two of them; for weeks I thought I was talking to the same person. In fact, I admit to having been a trifle confused when the neighbour I was chatting to one day had managed to sprout a moustache the next. It was then that I started having just the slightest suspicion that I was missing something.

When Koos indulgently tells me they are twins, I can't help asking why it is that every time I speak to one of them they only talk in the first person as if the other one doesn't exist.

Koos considers this phenomenon thoughtfully. "I suppose it's because they really are inseparable in both mind and spirit," he muses. "They simply think as one."

As I become accustomed to this two-in-one pair, I am finding them to be gentle, kindly and hopelessly acquisitive – but not in the materialistic sense; it is rather that they cannot resist collecting things. Bearing in mind that I find my own little *roef* incredibly compact and could in no way imagine sharing it with anyone else, I am astounded to learn that the 'brothers', as they are commonly known, live together in their clipper's *roef* and they don't even have the luxury of a wheelhouse. Their hold, however, is dedicated to their collection of motorbikes and bicycles.

The beauty of their situation is that one of the twins works for the local waste disposal contractor, and as a result he is in a position to pick up the most incredible cast-outs. "The things people throw away," he says, shaking a bewildered head as he shows me the mountain of accumulated treasure in their capacious hold.

I can hardly see one thing that is complete, such is the heap of piled-up machinery, but here and there I recognise certain legendary names: British Enfield, Triumph, Velocette, and some early French motorcycles from the thirties whose names I can't remember now. It is truly an Aladdin's cave for the two-wheeler enthusiast. What, I ask, do they intend to do with all of these wonderful pieces of history?

Jon – or is it Arjen? – looks at me with a puzzled expression. His eyes glaze over dreamily and his reply is no real answer at all. They have as much again stored at their mother's house, he tells me, and every weekend they go to there for both Sunday lunch and the chance to see the rest of their treasure.

These two are the ultimate squirrels. Very dear, kindly squirrels it is true, but they cannot bear to throw anything away, so I wonder what they will do if they keep on collecting at the same rate – buy another barge maybe? The clipper already takes up its full measure of the time they have to spend on maintenance, and each Sunday they carefully scrape and paint a few square centimetres each of its steelwork, or wash down one section of their deck each or wax a metre or two of their tarpaulin – each.

Then they have an ongoing project in the restoration of an old *"notaris"* boat and they spend another careful couple of hours each week making, welding or riveting small sections of steel to replace the lacework of rusted metal that most of the boat consists of. Everything they do is done with incredible attention to detail and takes the two of them twice as long as it would one less particular individual – like myself, for example.

If, then, they were to buy another barge for storage, this of course would have to be another piece of heritage which, in its turn, would need maintenance, and so the mounds of treasure within would continue to lie in cobwebs, despite the love and reverence in which they are held.

Still, they are the best neighbours I could wish for, and when I lie in bed on Sunday mornings I love hearing them talk to each other in their low muted exchanges. I can imagine that they are characters in a children's TV show, because their sing-song Rotterdam accent gives their words a special kind of friendly innocence that would fit in well on programmes for the very young.

On my other side lies a magnificent but sad looking *tjalk*. It is the life's work of André, its owner, who is painstakingly recreating the sturdy sailing barge it once was. At the moment it doesn't look like much, but Koos tells me the amount of work that has already been done has won it the Restoration Project of the Year award, and the fact that every section of the barge is being restored with authentic materials and methods says much for André's patience and dedication.

I must say I am quite happy with this arrangement, as there is a sizeable gap between the Hoop and the *tjalk*, so I am having a very peaceful life in my corner of the harbour.

It is not to last for long, though, as two things happen almost simultaneously. The first is when I am woken by the phone at 5.30 a.m. on a clear, sparkling summer's morning. It is Mireille's husband, asking me if I could come now and come quickly. The time has arrived for one of the next generation of barge dwellers to emerge.

Leaping out of bed I send Sisha flying, undignified and indignant, to the floor as I pull on whatever comes to hand and dash across the road to the Wijnhaven.

Mireille is in the early stages of labour and is still quite lucid and good humoured. I pile her into her own car and, with as much speed and as little uncalled for haste as I can muster, we head for the clinic, some eight kilometres away. I have never done an ambulance run before so I am unsure whether I should drive foot-flat and risk being stopped by the police, who could either deal me a heavy fine or else give me a blue flashing escort. Knowing my luck, it would be the former.

Thankfully it is early, so we arrive without a hitch and I offload the mother-to-be, her husband and the about-to-be-delivered baby into the hands of a capable nurse. Mireille smiles cheerfully at me as she is borne away, so I feel confident all will be well.

Back home again, I tumble into bed to catch another hour's sleep before going off to work, but even this is curtailed. I am rudely awakened by the second incident, announced by a heart stopping bang. Head pounding in shock and concern, I lie still trying to figure out what the Hoop has hit, where we are going and how big the hole might be. Then, before my poor sleep-befuddled brain has made some sense out of this muddle, there is another thud. Not so strong this time but enough to jolt me in my bed. Leaping up, I scramble up the stairs and look out of the wheelhouse windows.

I sigh, resignedly. The penny drops and all is now clear. Through the glass, I see the bows of a familiar barge edging alongside and then, as its stern levels with mine, I find myself looking at some very familiar teeth. I might have guessed. It is Philip, and he has brought his barge, the Tholen, to fill the gap between the Hoop and the *tjalk*. I should have known from the first bang that it could only have been him, steering in his 'parking by ear' fashion, and am reminded of one of the first occasions I saw him playing captain.

It was the previous year, when he was leaving the harbour on one of his other barges. I was watching from the railings next to the bridge, as was to become my custom. Seeing that it was about to be opened, Philip put the engine in forward gear and then, to my fascination, he disappeared below. The barge shot towards the bridge, which was now in the process of lifting, and I'm sure I was not the only one holding my breath or gasping with horror as his wheelhouse missed the steel girders of the support structure by a mere whisker. All I could think was that his guardian angel was doing overtime, because when he reappeared the danger was past. He just resumed his place at the wheel as if everything was completely normal, and was in fact totally oblivious to the collective sigh of relief that I swear I could hear whistling round the harbour.

As for his presence here this morning, I do vaguely remember him saying he needed to do some further work on his boat in the Oude Haven, and that he had to vacate the official work spot to make way for someone else, but I hadn't reckoned on him sneaking in here. It makes sense though, as the Hoop is full of his materials and tools, so it is an obvious place for him to moor up. Ah well, my landlord is good company and I couldn't ask for a more genial neighbour.

With my morning's peace now totally shattered, I go below to make some coffee and recover my equilibrium.

Koos and I are officially an item. Everyone else in the harbour maintains they have known for months so I suppose it's just as well that we now know it too. Not that it makes a significant difference to the way we live, as we still keep our own barges and have decided that the five or so craft that separate us keep things in healthy perspective.

This aside, the fact of the acknowledgement brings me some interesting new acquaintances. Suddenly, *liggers* I have never met before start greeting me as if I am an old friend. Others look at me with curiosity, perhaps realising that they had no idea I existed until they started seeing me with Koos, and even now they sometimes don't make the connection.

Just for fun one Sunday morning we take a first public stroll around the three harbours that make up our village. Walking arm in arm we are tickled by the idea that our dignified promenade could figure as a kind of 'state visit'. We have a hard time containing our laughter as we offer regal nods while we wave decorously to the friends and neighbours who see us passing and greet us enthusiastically. Nonetheless, it serves to confirm all the speculation and I feel that everyone can now relax and leave us to get on with things. It also means that there are number of new folk I too will have to greet in future.

Two additions to this list are Tom and his father Henk, both of whom live in the harbour but on different barges. Tom has twinkling eyes, an infectious smile, and the dark good looks of a Peruvian prince with his sleek black hair tied in a pony-tail. I believe his mother is actually Indonesian. Henk, on the other hand, is like many of the more 'mature' men in this community in that he still wears his curly hair long and looks as if the hippy days of the seventies have remained somehow suspended in time. Father and son are both kind, cheerful and very friendly, and it seems that the only problem they have is with each other.

Asking Henk about Tom, and vice versa, is likely to result in a lengthy list of complaints. Quite perversely, though, they have a distinct tendency to be attracted to the same women, which only generates further excuses for locking horns. All this apart, and quite ironically, they are unshakeably devoted to each other and can usually be found working together in apparently companionable silence on their respective barges – although, in truth, they may not actually be on speaking terms.

Henk is a master craftsman when it comes to woodwork and is renowned for his skill in making traditional *koekoeks*, entrance hatches and doors for the barges. He is a true artist who works in teak and other exotic materials and uses the traditional methods of joinery as well. Tom is currently attempting to follow in his father's footsteps by doing a course in boat carpentry and occasionally comes to drink tea with me and look at the progress I am making with my own woodwork. I am pleased by his interest but I suspect there is another motive that has a stronger influence on him than my ability with a chisel or saw. He has spotted Jodie, my daughter, visiting with some frequency; not so curiously, he often seems to turn up when she is with me. Fortunately for my own peace of mind, Henk doesn't appear to share his taste this time round.

Tom's barge is a very rare species indeed. It is called a *kraak* and is an iron-built sailing vessel of the 19th century. When he bought it, it was practically beyond repair and so rusted it had been discarded as a no-hoper by everyone else. He paid a nominal price for it but Koos tells me Tom himself should have been paid to take it, and that he deserves a medal for the work and restoration he has done to revive the old vessel. Painstakingly, he has replaced every rusted section, not by doubling the plates, which is what most people do, but by cutting out the offending parts and virtually 'stitching' new pieces in place with precise riveting. It is a work of art, and rather a shame that most of this impeccable craftsmanship is below the water line. If I were him, I would proudly offer the public the chance to dive below and take a look at my perfectly authentic patchwork – for a small fee of course.

The one thing that both amazes and appals me about Tom is that he lacks the one skill that most of us would consider vital before ever setting foot on a boat. When he isn't working on his barge, he crews for charter sailing ships and is an experienced, dedicated sailor, but the fact remains that he has never learnt to swim. He also confesses that he is always seasick for the first couple of days at sea, and so I find it hard to fathom how he has the courage to go out there at all. When I chide him about taking swimming lessons, he smiles at my indignation as if I am some kind of clucking old hen and says, "If it's my time to go, then so be it," in a way that is obviously designed to make me even more indignant – which it does, and so I continue to cluck, much to my own annoyance.

Tom and I quite often meet in the late evenings when I go for a shower in the office building at the yard. The busiest time for scrubbing up is usually around ten o'clock, so I tend to wait until closer to midnight. Tom seems to do the same, and I frequently have to wait for him to come out of the shower cubicle, or we wait together for one of the other occupants to finish. Mostly, I prefer to follow him as then I don't have to contend with the flooding on the floor that some of the others manage to leave in their enthusiasm to wash and go. We both mutter about this inconvenience, and I occasionally think there is a silent competition going on between us to see who can avoid being first.

There is quite a strong incentive among the *liggers* to install their own bathing facilities on board, as the shower room in the office is sometimes none too hygienic and I've found it is always wise to have the wherewithal to clean the floor tiles in my wash bag as well as the usual items. Any normal person would probably be rather disconcerted to see that my toiletries consist of a flannel, soap and nail brush packed closely together with scouring cream, a cloth and a bottle of industrial strength bleach. However, the latter are most definitely needed before I can safely and confidently use the former. In fairness, this is mostly because people with their barges on the slipway are obliged to use these wash rooms, and the process of scraping and painting a boat's bottom is not only hard work but also extremely dirty. They consequently tend to leave quite a lot of the evidence behind them.

Personal maintenance in this style feels somewhat like camping or doing youth hostels on a permanent basis but it has the advantage of being a remarkably effective way of getting to know people, and the hot water is free and plentiful. As a result I don't mind it at all, apart from the trek up to the yard and back. This can be embarrassing when, armed with towels and a wash bag decorated with a nodding yellow duck's head, I weave my way through the glamorously dressed partygoers thronging the quay outside the cafés. Even worse is when I have to return with my hair wrapped in said towel and the nodding duck swinging from one wrist. Girls in shiny satin give me blank eyed stares as they deliberately try not to see me. It feels rather like being at a formal dinner dance dressed in spotty pyjamas and oversized slippers. Nevertheless, I walk with an aplomb I don't feel. After all, this is our harbour and our home and I'm not prepared to sneak around like a rat in the night, but even so, my haughty air takes some resolve.

Mireille is back home with her baby daughter. I have been to see her a couple of times at the clinic which, I must say, was not my idea of a hospital at all. In the Netherlands it is quite customary for women to have their babies at home and hospital deliveries are confined to those with medical problems. In Mireille's case, her barge wasn't quite ready for the big day and, although her husband was working round the clock to get things finished, the attending midwife felt it would be altogether less stressful if the birth took place away from the construction site. To this end, Mireille was booked in at a clinic which is in fact one wing of the local airport hotel, and was furnished in exactly the same style as any small Holiday Inn might have been.

The charm of this system is that it is totally private and has all the benefits attached to being a paying guest, added to which the father can stay too if he wishes, and the couple can make the room their own home for the duration of their stay. When I visited Mireille, we lay together on the bed with the baby between us and watched television. It seemed a very civilised way of being hospitalised.

On her return, I slip round to her barge to see how she and little Noortje are adjusting to life without room service, and I find things much as I would expect. Mother Mireille exudes a calm contentment and a philosophical acceptance of her new status, while baby Noortje continues with the business of demand feeding without any apparent awareness of a change in surroundings. One bonus is that they do now have a bathroom complete with washing machine, thanks to the determined activities of the new dad during the period of Mireille's confinement, so the daily chores of early motherhood have at least been brought into line with twenty first century life.

Most of the relative newcomers to the harbour, myself included, are still coping with rather primitive conditions on our barges, and when one of our number announces the completion of a bathroom there is immediate and intense interest. Viewings are encouraged, methods are analysed and examined and then the equipment has to be demonstrated. Mireille's bathroom is of special interest because it has been constructed on a raised platform, underneath which are both the fresh water and foul water tanks. They have a real and normal flushing 'loo', which is quite a rarity on a barge as, mostly, I have found the rather special ship's toilets that are operated by a hand pump and use outboard water for flushing.

Space is normally quite an issue when it comes to installing kitchens and bathrooms, but with her huge old Amstel brewery barge this is not a problem for Mireille and her husband. They have far more room than average, even compared to a normal house or flat. I look wistfully at their spacious living and wonder if I will ever have even so much as a tiny shower in my *bijoux residence*.

This is a question that is not to occupy me for long, though, because when I return home, I see Philip sitting out on his deck, apparently enjoying the evening air. He is looking serious for once, even pensive. As I step on board, he calls out to me to join him and, while I settle into a chair with a glass of wine in hand, he gives me the bad news.

He is going to put the Hoop up for sale, he says, watching earnestly for my reaction. He wants to go travelling and he has too many barges so he feels he should scale down and focus on getting his Tholen properly equipped.

"I'll never have the time to convert the Hoop for 'live-aboard', and I'm never going to live in it myself, so there's no point in keeping it," he tells me regretfully.

I gulp inwardly. The seriousness of Philip's intent is supported by the fact I have not seen his famous teeth throughout his explanation; he hasn't smiled – not even once. I am silent under the weight of his words, until he breaks the spell as quickly as he has cast it.

"But you don't need to worry just yet, Val," he comforts me. "It might take months before I sell it, so there's no great hurry. After all, I want a lot of money for the Hoop, so it won't be going overnight." And then, much to my absurd relief, the teeth gleam at me as his smile widens; suddenly the world seems in balance again.

CHAPTER TEN
Not A Hoop

It is taking some time for the reality of Philip's news to sink in, but the only thing I know for sure is that I will have to start looking for alternative accommodation. I have immersed myself so deeply in the character and confines of the Hoop that at the moment it seems beyond me to imagine living anywhere else. It has become my world, and I have adjusted myself to its limitations like a goldfish to its bowl.

Koos's Luxor has considerably more space than I have, but even so, it is too small for two people and besides, we rather like our current status of 'living together apart'. We start discussing what I should do, as I have certain requirements. I want to continue living on the water; I would also like to live in something with history, and without being too far from the harbour and all the friends I have made. A little more space would be desirable but I don't need that much so I won't be looking for a mansion – not that I have the means for one in any event. On the other hand, the idea of an apartment fills me with alarm. Just the thought of all those neighbours gives me instant claustrophobia. I sigh inwardly. I have been so lucky with the Hoop because house boats (*woonboten*) to rent are not easy to come by.

The answer is obvious when put like this. I will have to try and buy a barge of my own.

The next issue is where to start looking. To qualify for a place in the Oude Haven, my first choice of location, it will have to be either already historic or a worthy restoration project. This could be difficult as, although I like working with my hands, my skills are limited so I can't undertake too much in the way of steel work or structural change. There is also the question of money. I have some savings but not the kind of funds to buy a finished barge.

Narrowing down the options doesn't take much time then. What I have to look for is either a barge with an original exterior and everything to be done inside, or I should do what Koos has done and find something like a *dekschuit* to convert.

My spirits start to rise again with this new challenge. The searching is going to be as much fun as the satisfaction of finding. I try to push thoughts of leaving the Hoop out of my mind and focus on the new and exciting task of seeking out the right barge to suit me. Although I am aware there is no great rush, something tells me I shouldn't wait to be caught unprepared, so I'd better start the process now.

Buying magazines is one good source of information about boats for sale. Koos and I take to poring over endless pages of thumbnail advertisements with tiny, barely visible pictures until we realise there is not much to be gained from straining our eyes and curiosity to this degree.

We then move on to the Internet. I don't have a connection on board, although I do now have a phone line, but Koos uses the web frequently and knows all the good sites. He finds a few craft that seem to be worth further investigation, and so we plan a trip to go and view them.

The weather is still exceptionally fine and while August in the Netherlands is notoriously unreliable, we are being blessed with day after day of hot, bright sunshine. The clouds are so high and rare, they seem to be more like random fluff balls drifting close to the sky's limit. There is a slight haze on the horizon on the morning of our first trip, but the air is singing with life and it feels great to be heading out of the city on an adventure to track down my barge. I ponder on that a moment. My barge. It has a good sound.

We are driving our battered little Renault 5. We've had it a month or two now after buying it cheap from a friend, and while its motor is still gutsy and strong, the bodywork is showing signs of strain. It also has no speedometer, so we have to guess how fast we are driving which can be slightly unnerving whenever we see or pass a police car. There is always a risk that our method of testing speed – a thumb suck to the breeze – may be slightly inaccurate.

Nothing daunted, though, we head eastwards on our first mission. We have a map, but Koos says he knows the way, so I trust his judgement. Our quest is to view two boats that we have seen advertised. Both are 'fixer-uppers', but we are keeping open minds, as the descriptions given by brokers are not to be taken too literally. A barge 'ready for conversion' is just as likely to be a barge ready for its last trip – to the scrap yard.

The address we have been given for our first visit is at a shipyard, which sounds promising, but when we eventually find it the yard in question is on a remote stretch of river which is none too accessible. We have to bump our way down a sandy track, the end of which opens out into a bare patch of scrub land beside the yard itself. Looking in through the open doorway, the work in progress seems to be devoted entirely to building new craft. It also appears to be deserted, except for some sounds of metallic banging coming from somewhere at the rear.

We make our way past the skeleton of a new hull until by following the sound of scraping and hammering we find its source. There are two young men working together on the new construction, but there is no one else. The air is heavy with the heat, and the whole place has a feeling of desolation about it. The men regard us with expressionless eyes and no curiosity and I wonder if there is anyone home behind their motionless features. It makes me slightly uneasy, but Koos is undaunted and approaches them with his courteous charm, asking them about the boat we have seen advertised.

They are immediately transformed and, with smiling animation, one of them leads the way to a spot outside where we see an old hull above our heads, supported by a kind of cradle. We have to climb up the wall next to it to take a look and, as soon as we see its superstructure, we know it is not the one.

It is some kind of small *beurtschip* (local delivery barge) but it is far too decrepit for one thing, and the hold is much too low. There is so much rust in the deck and cabin, you can see straight though it in several places and the timber of the hatch boards is completely rotten. The amount of work that would be needed to create a decent live-aboard barge would also disqualify it completely from a place in the Oude Haven.

Regretfully, we clamber down again and Koos explains to the young yard workers that the boat is not what we are looking for. Their faces revert again to those eerily blank masks and we hurriedly thread our way back through the accumulated machinery in the yard, and out again into the sunshine. Rattling our way back along the track between tall, dry grasses, I feel a sense of relief at having escaped in one piece. Ridiculous, I know, but the shipyard and its occupants have given me a severe dose of the creeps.

Our next port of call is equally remote and I marvel that in such an overcrowded country there are these small 'outbacks' that seem to be so removed from the modern world. The barge we want to see has to be viewed from the banks of the river and to reach it we have to park in a lay-by and hike across a couple of fields, which also happen to be home to a herd of placidly curious cows.

Unfortunately I am not dressed for rambling in the meadows as, just for once, I am wearing a loose and long flowing skirt with thonged sandals – not exactly ideal wear for thrashing though clumps of rich and virulently green stinging nettles.

I eye the cows; they are apparently watching us to see what we are going to do, meditatively chewing their cud in the process. Then I squint at the nettles. Can I get through them before the cows get to me? Positioning Koos in front of me to do the beating I follow his tracks across the field, keeping a nervous eye on the bovine regiment that is now marching steadily and irrevocably towards us. As our pace quickens, so does theirs. Ours quickens still further; the cows follow our lead. By the time we are making a final dash for the trees lining the river bank, the herd is thundering across the plain in pursuit. All right, I accept this might be just a slight exaggeration, but then I have to acknowledge that I am living proof of the difference between a cow and a coward.

Harmless though they might be, I have no desire to be trampled underfoot by several hundred tons of cattle, and I've no doubt that their brakes are not that good once they are pounding along at full speed. I am consequently drenched with a flood of relief when we slither down the bank to the safety of the water's edge. Even Koos looks happy to be on the safe side of the trees. The cows, however, regard us with disappointment and, one by one, they shuffle round to go back to their core business – chewing cud and making milk.

Having wiped the sweat from my eyebrows and the twigs and grass seeds from between my toes, I look out into the river to see if I can identify the 'renovator's dream' that we have braved the wilds to view. Koos is already scanning the stretch of water, and his expression is not encouraging.

"Hmm," he mutters "there's only one water borne object here that can be described as a barge, and it's that."

I follow the direction of his pointing finger and gaze at the floating wreck over to the right that I have just moments before been discounting.

It is nothing more than an old hulk of rotting steel and timbers. The photo on the internet must have been from its good side, but from what I can see from here there is nothing good about any of it. How anyone could have the courage to take on the restoration of such a collection of rusting rivets and planks I do not know. It is also moored against a couple of poles about ten metres from the bank, so there is no possibility of getting any closer to find out if we are being overly pessimistic.

Disappointed, we turn around and look for a way back to the car that won't challenge our pastoral friends to another bout of 'chase the Charlies.' Turning to the right, we follow the bank along until the edge of the cows' field is in view. It is marked by a barbed wire fence and its safe side is a stretch of grassy land that separates the field from the track where we have parked the car. The only thing we have to do is find a way through another two strand barbed wire fence which, for some unfathomable reason, has been erected along the river bank. The only place we can find is a spot where the bottom strand has broken between two fence poles, and we can crawl through into a lovely juicy clump of nettles.

Koos's look is question enough, and my answering grimace tells him anything is better than braving the cloven-hoofed monsters again. Koos goes through the gap first, and gallantly lays his coat down across the worst of the nettles. Then, wrapping my own jacket round my hands, I creep through after him. Squashing the nettles as I go, I emerge on the other side with burning ankles and tangled hair, but otherwise unharmed. I should have known in advance, though. Country walks are never the idyllic rambles of films and books. There are always thorns, nettles and barbed wire fences, and for some reason they are always most evident when I decide to don a dress and do the feminine thing. The end result means I nearly always illustrate to perfection the concept of being 'dragged through a hedge backwards'. Perhaps I should simply accept the fact that 'well groomed' and 'gracious elegance' will never be words that are synonymous with me – but then maybe this is just as well, given the way of life I have chosen.

After this somewhat abortive trip I find it difficult to raise quite so much enthusiasm for going on ship-seeking adventures, although I am aware that I need to keep looking. Philip has given the Hoop's details to an agent, but it will not be actively marketed until he has done some necessary repairs and put some windows in the top of the hold, so I don't need to feel too pressurised just yet.

In the meantime, I keep browsing through the various brokers' sites on the Internet. It is rather a dangerous pursuit, though, as I often see the most beautiful barges with gorgeous interiors, but which also have equally stunning price tags. I haven't really decided what I'm looking for yet. The main criteria are that it shouldn't be too long, as I want to be able to manage it myself. A wheelhouse would be a plus but isn't essential, and it would be preferable to have a motor barge rather than a sailing vessel, mainly because I have no intention of going anywhere without the comforting growl of a good diesel engine beneath my feet. What's more, open waters hold no appeal for me whatsoever and my dreams are always of sneaking off down quiet, tree shrouded canals where the only ripples are caused by rising fish and the backwash from my boat.

When we went to Den Haag for the festival, the beauty of the *westlanders* caught my attention, and so now I am keeping my eyes open for a possible candidate for conversion among these charming craft. They are mostly found as recreational sailing barges, but I have seen one or two motor *westlanders* and I love the idea of building one of them up in a similar style to Koos's Luxor.

There are several available for sale and they seem to be very reasonably priced, but all those I have seen advertised have been modernised and improved beyond repair. Finding one that is still in its original state is both more challenging and inevitably more costly.

Nonetheless, the harbour grapevine bears fruit once again, and Koos drops in to tell me about a *westlander* that is apparently lying in affordable decrepitude in Delfshaven, the only harbour with any genuine history in Rotterdam.

We drive across the city early on Sunday morning. It is unexpectedly grey and chilly with a damp mist clinging to leaves, coats and hair, beading them with moisture. It is also incredibly hushed, which gives an eerie stillness to the day that, somewhat illogically, makes us whisper. We park in a small side street near Delfshaven and walk round into the harbour as the church bell of the Oude Kerk is clanging in a solitary, almost ominous rhythm that jars with the muffled quiet of the morning.

Turning the corner, I am struck anew by the charm of the harbour. Delfshaven lies at the entrance to the waterway to Delft and the heart of old Holland. Even the name evokes history. It was here that the Pilgrim Fathers, a group of protestant clergy, held their last service in the Oude Kerk before fleeing certain persecution from their Catholic overlords. The year was 1620. They crossed the Channel to Southampton in the Speedwell and there met up with more of their kind before setting sail from Plymouth to America on the Mayflower.

The streets on each side of the water are cobbled but grass creeps through the cracks between them. There are tiny shops filled with art, bric-a-brac of the fifties, old books and cottage furniture. There are cafés, quaint pubs and intimate restaurants, and the atmosphere is enhanced by the graceful masts of the sailing barges that line the quays.

I catch my breath as if we have somehow entered a secret world whose spell will be broken if we so much as breathe a word. Walking softly towards the end of the harbour, the unnaturally loud clatter of a man and his dog crossing the small lifting bridge shakes us out of our reverie, and the man greets Koos with a cheery "*goede morgen*".

At the southern end of the harbour the character changes because the older buildings have been replaced by modern terraced houses, but there is still the original windmill, standing proud and erect in its place at the end of the quay.

We are at this point because this is apparently where we will find the *westlander* that's worth seeing. There are several smaller craft tied up in front of us and most of them are modern cruisers, 'tupperware boats', as we irreverently call them, with the typical snobbery of historic barge owners. Truth be told, the owners of small pleasure boats have as much fun, if not more, than we do and much less maintenance, so we haven't got that much to crow about – except that our barges are undoubtedly more romantic and graceful.

Looking up and down the line of boats, there is only one *westlander* moored here, but it doesn't fit the description we've been given at all. Certainly not original, it has a steel superstructure with windows cut out of the sides and looks very much like a project in progress. Koos murmurs his puzzlement and we stand a moment, wondering what to do.

Looking out over the end of the quay beyond the windmill, there is an open expanse of water that extends to the west. It makes a T-crossing at the end of yet another harbour that lies parallel to Delfshaven, called the Achterhaven. Moving past the mill, we see a boat moored just round the corner at the end of the Achterhaven which looks very much like a *westlander* from where we are standing, although it is too far to make out more than just the general shape.

Retracing our steps, we head back to the first lane that cuts through the houses to the Achterhaven beyond. The street into which we turn is in every way as picturesque as its better-known neighbours in Delfshaven, but the opposite side of the water here is bleak and decrepit and there are no quaint shops with tantalising artefacts on show. The boats in these berths are mostly larger cruisers and very *un*-historic converted barges; all the same, I can imagine it might be quite peaceful to live here without the tourist traps and guided tours prompted by those renegade clergymen of long ago.

Crossing a newly built footbridge, I am momentarily distracted by the large, rather grandiose building at its other end. On closer inspection, there is a notice proclaiming this to be the original warehouse of the VOC (*Verenigde Oostindische Compagnie*), the East India Company on which so much of the Netherland's trading wealth was built. It intrigues me that this building stands alone and apparently rather unloved on this far side of the harbour. It has an abandoned appearance but is currently used by the film industry and is most definitely classified as a monument. It seems a shame to see it so neglected.

We walk on past it to an area of waste ground where grass and weeds compete for dominance. It is fenced in and we realise that we cannot reach the quay where the boat lies as there is no path around the edge. Peering round the corner, it is clear we have found our goal. The pretty scooped bows of the Westlander are distinctive, but we still can't see the rest of it.

Koos scours the perimeter of the fence till he finds a hole large enough for me to crawl through. Being a hero, and athletic, he of course vaults over the top. Thrashing our way through the tall soaked grasses, I am smugly pleased I am properly kitted out today in boots and jeans, but it is still wet work to reach the quay.

Looking down onto the little barge, however, it seems as if it has been a wasted trip. Disappointment washes over me when I see its state of decay. Apart from anything the hold is much too low and raising it would throw all the proportions out, but besides this there is a great deal of repair work to be done on the steel hull. It must have been a lovely barge at one time, though. Its lines are so graceful and the length is ideal. I am still inclined to look for one that would suit me but I'll just have to accept that the hunt is going to take more time. This one is not the answer to anyone's dreams.

Last night, while poring over ever more boating magazines with Sisha simultaneously trying to knead them into a nest, I spotted what looked like a little gem. It is an authentic motor *westlander* with a nicely old-fashioned conversion to the hold using planking in a similar style to the Luxor's, except that this one is painted white, and has windows and a smart red door at one end. The hull looks very well maintained and the crimson stripe painted around it gleams richly in the photo. It doesn't take much to persuade Koos that we should go and take a look at it, as it is moored at Vlaardingen, a small fishing port that is now one of Rotterdam's satellite towns. According to the advertisement the boat comes with its own *ligplaats* (berth) at a wonderfully meagre rate.

We head out of the city early to avoid what threatens to be a hot day, and a quick twenty minutes later we are pulling off the highway at the Vlaardingen exit. It is surprisingly green given the proximity to Europe's largest port and one of Shell's most important refineries across the river at Pernis. The directions lead us to the outskirts of the town where the canal from the harbour becomes more rural, and boats are moored sporadically along the side amongst reeds and undergrowth. After parking the car we walk along the towpath heading further into the country, and then, just before a bridge, we find the *westlander*.

It is indeed a little gem, so clean, so brightly painted and with the particularly attractive stern that a motor barge uniquely has.

But, little is the operative word. It is only fourteen metres long, and the living space is just over half of that. With its narrow beam of under three metres at its widest point, the maximum space I would ever be able to have is a very modest nineteen square metres. The interior is pleasantly panelled and includes a double bed, toilet, tiny kitchen and table, but no space for a shower whatsoever. The engine, however, is huge for so small a barge and takes up a disproportionate amount of room.

I love it, but in my heart I know it's not right for me. In fact it would give me even less space than I have on the Hoop overall, and that would be poverty. My heart says yes, but my head and Koos both say no.

Back on the towpath I pace up and down, studying its lean lines and conformation in the hopes I can come up with a plan to make it feasible to extend the accommodation, but all my ideas involve ruining what is in fact a charming complete barge which should be left as it is. Sighing with regret, we do just that and head back to the car.

On the return journey, Koos tells me that the great search will have to be put on hold for a while as two events are coming up which will require his dedicated attention and – with his eyes asking the question – hopefully some of mine too.

Next week, the Luxor is going on the slipway to have its bottom scrubbed and painted, something I have already promised to help with, and then, at the beginning of September, we are leaving for an event in Lille, a journey which will take the best part of a week and will be my first long trip as skipper's mate. There is thus plenty to keep us both occupied for the next few weeks and, despite my impatience, I will have to resume my quest for the perfect *woonboot* at a later stage. I can only hold thumbs that Philip doesn't sell my current home before I've found another equally worthy of my devotion.

CHAPTER ELEVEN
On The Slips

Anyone living on a barge will be only too familiar with the anxiety of waiting for the insurance inspector to come and do a thickness testing.

The thing with having a floating home is that water outside is good – in fact, wonderful – but water inside is very, very bad. On the whole, old Dutch barges have hulls of steel or iron and, of course, over time normal degradation and wear causes the metal to get pitted and thin in patches. Added to this, and if care isn't taken, condensation inside the hull will cause rust to form on the flat bottom of the barge, which can be an even greater problem. With corrosion attacking from both sides, it's only a matter of time before one meets the other, and that old sinking feeling starts to take hold.

The worst-case scenario is when the steel becomes so thin it only takes a few taps from the Insurance inspector's hammer to create a hole. Not only will this probably be very expensive, it can be quite devastating for the owners. All their confidence in their barge is likely to be terminally shattered by a single strike of the hammer, putting an end to the days of carefree faring. From this moment on, every trip carries with it the burden of the "what if" factor, such as: what if there's a spot the inspector missed? Or, what if we hit something on the spot the inspector missed? Or worse still, what if we hit another ship on the spot the inspector missed? I won't go on, but I'm sure the message is clear. It is a heavy burden indeed.

To prevent such a dent to the spirits and the bank balance, barges have to be inspected by the insurance company every six years, and this is called a *keuring*. It is actually the boating equivalent of a car's certificate of roadworthiness, although the period between checks is much longer. However, most bargees think it wiser to take their boats out of the water every two or three years to clean the bottom, check them for pits and do any interim repairs. They then paint them thickly with a protective underwater coating, which helps to prevent further deterioration for the next couple of years or until the next *hellingbeurt*, the Dutch term for a spell on the slipway.

There are plenty of other reasons for taking a barge out of the water as well. Sometimes modifications need to be done to the propeller, or the owners may want a bow thruster installed. This is an engine with its own propeller, which is placed in a tube inserted in a hole cut into the barge's bows below the water line. Many skippers, both professional and amateur, wouldn't set sail without one as they make such a difference to control and handling, especially of the larger barges. In effect, you can steer at both ends.

Today, it is the Luxor's turn on the slips, but only for a *keuring* and a clean-up. The Inspector is coming later this afternoon, so we are going up with the early high tide. We have to get the bottom clean and dry before he comes with his dreaded hammer. It is well before seven in the morning and nearly the end of August, so the days are already getting shorter. The light is just seeping through the sky and there is a ghostly feel to the dawn as we quietly cast off the ropes and pull slowly back into the still waters of the harbour.

Nothing is moving. There is hardly any traffic on the main road yet, and only the odd cyclist swishes past over the bridge into the Haringvliet, a blurred silhouette in the half-light. The silence seems to have an almost tangible substance and even our own breathing is a rude intrusion into this secret world.

We come to a standstill about twenty metres from the slipway, as we have to wait for last week's occupants to come down first. For some reason it is taking time to organise so we float, waiting in the hush of the morning, talking softly. One by one, the various harbour lights go out as the daylight increases. Then, and with an almost shocking suddenness, the street lamps blink out. But still we wait, and watch the sun rise in the sky.

It is nearly an hour before the *werf* is clear and we can make our way to a position across four of the five ramps that form the slipway. The Luxor is tied to two poles to ensure it stays in position until the trolleys that move up each ramp are at a point where the bottom of the barge sits on their flat surfaces. They then continue to make their laborious way up the ramps taking the Luxor with them. All told, the procedure takes about ten minutes.

It feels as if we are high above the rest of the world now, although in fact we are only two metres or so above the concrete base of the work area, and even less over the actual ground level. Still, when you are used to actually sitting in the water and looking up at the world around you, this relatively insignificant height seems enormous.

The next step is to put the yard's *loopplank* in position. Since this is a massive, heavy gangway, it needs mechanical power to lift it into place. Bertus hoists himself up into the harbour crane's little cubicle from where this almost historic machine is operated. A heavy chain with two chunky hooks is attached to each side of the *loopplank*, which is lying on the ground. Lifting it slowly, one of the harbour assistants, Wally, holds on to the end of the plank and manoeuvres it into position at the side of the barge, where its own hooks are placed over the rim. The *loopplank* is then lowered to the ground and the hooks are released. We can now go ashore.

First stop is a cup of coffee in the office, a ritual that is obligatory for all slipway tenants. Bertus makes a fairly potent brew, guaranteed to get the juices going and the blood buzzing, and which certainly helps with the long day ahead. We sit on the basic steel-framed chairs that are set round the walls of the small, cosy office. Bertus holds court and regales everyone with stories of his own background in the great ship and steel yards of yesteryear. I don't follow too much of it as I am quite tired, so I just smile benignly and hope that no one says anything to me that I will be expected to answer.

The next step is to clean the bottom of the Luxor. It is covered in a thick layer of tiny mussels and weed that have attached themselves to the steel and proliferated in an almost disgustingly healthy fashion. They clearly didn't have too much to do down there except breed and 'muscle' in on each other.

We grab spades and start to scrape. Standing underneath the barge, it looks huge and the work is all above our heads, which makes it tough on the arms and neck. The task seems daunting, but that's not the worst part. After a mere minute or two I shake myself free of a fine crop of shells and indescribable muck, and go to dress myself properly. No one has told me that this job is like showering yourself in rather ripe smelling fish well mixed with cold, wet gravel. Given the fact that it is probably the worst punishment I personally could be subjected to, particularly as regards my olfactory senses, I am not all that amused. I return covered from head to toe in yellow PVC, gloved, goggled and virtually muzzled, to finish the job.

Nevertheless, the next stage has rather more dire effects. We have to wash the barge's bottom clean with a high-pressure hose. I am already well kitted out, but Koos has to do the same, and we take it in turns to blast the final shells, weed and dirt from the Luxor's underside. I go to it with a will as this is fun and the water jet obliterates everything it meets. After about an hour, Koos taps me on the shoulder to show he is happy with the result and yes, I can stop now. In fact I *should* stop now and no, I can't go on. Why not? Well, it's not necessary and more importantly, it's expensive. Aha, the crux of the matter at last. This is Holland after all.

I stop, but feel quite sorry to be leaving it here. Maybe everyone should have a spell at doing this, as I can well believe it's a great de-stresser. All you have to do is imagine that all your worst obstacles, enemies and frustrations are being systematically blasted away. It is a truly cleansing experience – internally at any rate.

The external experience is the reverse. Peering at myself in the small mirror above the basin in the office toilet, I am entertained by my transformation into a raccoon. Without my goggles, there are two large, circular white patches around my eyes. The rest of my face is black, and the smell coming off my overalls would certainly be instant allure to any raccoon worth its salt, or maybe rather to a skunk.

Unluckily for me, another thing no one has told me is that the old tar-based paint that skippers used to put on their barge's bottoms can give some people quite bad allergic reactions. Apparently, I am one of them. The first symptoms are a tightening of the skin that feels rather like sunburn. I wash my face and neck thoroughly, but the burning feeling grows, and I notice that my cheeks are beginning to look red. The feeling of everything stretching worsens and when I look in the mirror again an hour or so later I have made a further transformation from raccoon to chipmunk. If it didn't hurt so much by now, I'd be laughing, but in fact I'm now in quite a lot of pain and don't know what to do.

The harbour wives come to the rescue. They each have their own tried and tested remedies, which are undoubtedly more effective than anyone else's. Mireille gives me a tube of lanolin cream with the reasonable suggestion that if it's good for nappy rash, it will probably be good for me too. I ponder for a moment on the comparison of my face with a baby's bottom and make a conscious decision not to dwell on that. Frits's girlfriend José gives me a bottle of calamine. This is no doubt very cooling, but when it dries, it makes me look like an old and withered geisha girl, caked with cracked powder – not quite the impression I'm keen on fostering, especially as it doesn't seem to make too much difference to the furious flushed feeling.

In fact, despite all the kind and well-meant remedies, nothing works and my poor face continues to swell further and suffer more. The sunshine makes it worse too, so I take to wearing a wide brimmed hat, which only serves to increase the eccentricity of my appearance. Neither does it help when I come upon Philip and other friends sitting in the office and they all start laughing; the trouble being that I want to laugh too, but it hurts too much.

This aside, the insurance inspector arrives in the middle of the afternoon. The bottom of the barge is completely dry thanks to the hot sunshine, so he gets to work with his hammer and his chalk. Tapping with an air of studied concentration, he covers sections of the boat's hull below the waterline. Drawing lines with chalk, he marks the spots he would like to test, and Koos follows him round with an angle grinder, zealously polishing the areas that have been identified for thickness testing.

From what we have gleaned so far it doesn't look too bad, and even the inspector is still smiling. Of course it's possible he gets a perverse delight in finding fault, but even so, Koos is optimistic that there won't be too much to do; maybe just the odd 'sticking plaster' here and there.

I decide to take a break and brave the shops. We still need to eat, so it seems like a good moment to leave the inspector to Koos's anxious care and do something about my own maintenance. When I return the verdict will either be good or bad, so it's a fifty-fifty chance either way. I just hope for Koos's sake that it is good since with the trip to Lille on the horizon he doesn't need any major hold ups at this stage.

Leaving the comfort zone of the harbour for the normal world is an intimidating experience in my present condition. At the supermarket, I feel like some kind of flashing beacon. My face is so red and swollen, and I look so bizarre in my floppy hat and dungarees, that the other rather well-bred and well turned-out shoppers manage to forget their equally well-schooled manners for a moment and stare at me openly as I pass with my trolley. I may as well have dropped in on them from the Australian outback, and I think I should definitely be chewing on a stem of grass.

Still, I pretend to ignore them and carry on with the job in hand. There are certain priorities when you are 'on the *helling*'. The first of these is to make sure there is enough coffee and biscuits, not only for yourself but for any of the harbour dwellers who come wandering through the yard to have a look at what you are doing and give you the benefit of their undoubtedly more expert opinion. This can range from what kind of paint you should be using for the bottom to which parts of the barge should be repaired, modified or otherwise adjusted according to their own convictions.

The next essential for the shopping trolley is beer – the reasons being the same as those for the coffee, but for rather later in the day when the work is done. All the inspecting, gesticulating and peering can then be done with the help of a half-litre of good Dutch pils. Such sessions can go on until darkness obscures all but the wink of the beer cans' shiny surface in the moonlight as they are waved around at the end of invisible arms.

Only after these vital supplies have been loaded into the trolley can I get down to the business of buying food. This is mostly for the ingredients needed for easy-to-make one-pot pasta or stew dishes that can be left to simmer while the cleaning up is done. Then there must be plenty of bread for lunchtime sandwiches of the doorstep variety, as painting ships is hungry work. Good fillings to create the doorsteps are required too.

By the time I have trundled my way round all the aisles I have a full load. The challenge for me now is how I'm going to balance it all on my bike, which is all I've brought with me as transport. The checkout girl makes sympathetic noises about my face, so I just tell her it's an allergy, the Dutch word for which is almost the same as it is in English. If you say it with a guttural 'g', you can't go far wrong, and it even sounds quite impressive, as the shop girl's amazed look testifies.

Wheeling my trolley outside, I start to pile the shopping onto my bike. I have *fietstasjes* (saddle bags) so they are the first to be filled. Next I strap the trays of beer onto the little rack behind the seat, and then I hang a carrier bag from each handle bar. I'm now ready to wobble my way home again. It isn't too far, but the carrier bags swing unnervingly, so after a few near misses with other cyclists I get off and walk the rest of the way – a much safer option, especially for the beer.

Back at the yard I find Koos in earnest discussion with Frits. The insurance man has packed up and gone, leaving one or two problems behind him. Koos is looking serious. Apparently, the hull needs quite a large patch over a thin spot on the water line just in front of the propeller. This is just about the worst place it could be as it is an awkward shape, for at this particular point the ship is all curves. The steel patch will have to be very carefully formed and bent into position, which could take some time.

Apart from this there isn't too much else to do; just another small patch over a pitted spot in the bottom, and a few rivets that need to be welded. Up until the 1950s, or thereabouts, all the sheets of steel on old barges were riveted together rather than welded, which was a later development. In the course of time the rivets themselves degenerate and can eventually be in danger of popping out, leaving neat but worrisome holes. As a result, when excessive wear on a rivet is spotted the solution is to weld it into place so that it can't come out – ever.

From what I gather, Frits is going to help with the welding as he is known to be patient and precise when it comes to these fiddly jobs. Quite apart from that, Koos likes working with him because he shares his ideas so readily and is more than willing to discuss different possibilities. Given the time limitation, they will get to work tomorrow and focus their attention solely on completing these urgent jobs. Although they are not major problems, we cannot go to Lille without having them done, because if anything were to go wrong the insurance would not cover any loss or damage at all.

My job will be to start painting the bottom. I stand at the bows and look down the length of the boat. It is what the Dutch call a *platbodem,* meaning it has no keel and is as flat as an enormous tray underneath. Words like 'daunting' and 'endless' spring to mind when I look at the expanse of steel that has to be painted. In fact, it is quite small as barges go – only twenty-two metres from stem to stern. Nonetheless, from where I'm standing it looks enormous, and I have to paint the whole thing – not once but at least twice, and preferably three times.

Ah well, I can't back out now, and I realise rather inconsequentially that the six-month trial period I promised myself when I came back last December is well and truly past. I haven't even thought of it until this moment, but it is suddenly and forcefully borne in on me that the option of withdrawal has now gone. Reflecting briefly on the situation, I also realise I don't mind and that I am now committed.

With this decision made, I pick up a paint roller. I am ready to get on with it.

By the end of the day's work I have covered half of the bottom with its first coat of the gooey black paint that is the modern substitute for tar. It still has a powerful tar-type smell, and I feel as if I've been impregnated with the stuff. My face burns even brighter. Maybe it isn't just the old paint that I'm allergic to.

Getting up for the second day of work, I notice that my skin has started to blister. This is going to be fun. Not only is it still swollen, red and tight, but now I'm going to look as if I'm desiccating. The mirror on the Hoop does nothing to soften the gruesome spectacle but, after smothering myself with a concoction of all the remedies I've been given, it does at least feel less painful. I can also quite truthfully tell all my generous donors that I have tried their remedies, although identifying which one is doing any good might be a challenge, given my methods. After feeding a yowling and totally unsympathetic Sisha, I am ready for the day. Donning my hat with a will, I set off to join Koos, who has already left for the yard.

When I descend the steps to the work area, Frits and Koos are busy making a template of the patch that will be placed next to the propeller. I am interested to see they are just using cardboard from an old box which, being flexible, they can push into the curves. Once they have drawn an outline of the shape, they can cut it out and transfer the template to a piece of steel. It looks rather simplistic but in fact this method is the ideal way to get the correct size of the patch that is needed. The hard part will be when they have to bend the steel to fit it snugly into place.

I retrieve my rollers from the buckets of water in which they have been standing overnight. It isn't necessary to clean them out every day as long as they are kept wet. The excess water is rolled out of them on a steel grid that sits over a special soak-away filled with sand. This filters out the water from all the nasty stuff very effectively and is used to dispose of much of the oily waste that results from these barge maintenance jobs. The paint bucket is still half full and I still have two and a half times the Luxor to paint so, with some rather reluctant resolve, I get to work again.

Push, pull, push pull. The rhythm of the roller threatens to become hypnotic at times, and only the fact that I have to make sure I fill in all the minute pits in the hull prevents me from becoming an automaton; that and the fact that my neck feels as if it is being progressively screwed into my shoulders and is objecting fiercely. I am very glad it is the Luxor and not the Hoop though, as then I would have five metres more to paint.

By lunchtime of the second day, I am proud to announce to the men folk that the whole of the bottom has a first coat, apart from the places that have to have their steel patches applied, of course. Koos and Frits merely nod in acknowledgement and carry on with the job of bending a stubborn piece of steel. I am deflated and disappointed. It seemed like such an achievement five minutes ago, but now I have to admit it isn't that much to brag about. What's more, all I'm likely to get is a bawdy chuckle from anyone else if I go around boasting that I've just finished painting my bottom. Ah well. Time for lunch and a break anyway.

In the afternoon, it starts to rain and the water runs in small rivulets down the side of the Luxor's hull. I can only give the flat part of the underside a second coat. When I have finished, I stop to take a look at what Frits and Koos are doing.

They have the partially prepared section of steel in place by the propeller and one side of it is spot-welded onto the hull. The other side is being pinioned by means of a special jack designed for holding things in position above the head. The Dutch word for this wonderful tool is a *dommekracht*, meaning dumb strength, so it's a bit like having a brainless version of Atlas to hold up your world. Every few minutes, Frits attacks the new steel patch with a small sledge hammer, which he then passes back to Koos while he welds the part he has been beating at one or two critical points to fix it securely. This process is repeated several times over for about an hour and, with a steady rhythm and patience, another side is finally spot welded into place.

It is exhausting work, and as I watch I realise my paint-rolling is child's play by comparison. Not only does this skill need endurance and strength, but patience, precision and artistry as well. Considering that all the welding has to be done while looking through a darkened perspex screen to protect the welder's eyes, my admiration for these masters grows in leaps.

It takes another day before this particular piece is finally finished, hammered mercilessly into following the natural curve of the hull. However, once the first part of the job has been completed, Frits has to weld neat, unbroken seams along all four sides of the patch, as it must be totally sealed. Even the tiniest pin-prick of a hole would produce an impressive flow of water into the barge once it is sitting back in the harbour and under pressure.

The last step is Koos's work. He follows the seams with a small chisel-ended hammer and removes any residue or protrusions, just to be finally sure that there are no weak spots or breaks in the neatly pleated flow of the weld. The process reminds me forcibly of icing a cake, except that it is much harder and more dangerous.

The next few days follow a similar pattern. I paint, Frits and Koos cut, hammer and weld, the rhythm only being broken by coffee breaks when we sit round the trestle table on the yard and get our next infusion of caffeine. Then, at the end of each day, I bring out the beer so that Koos and Frits can mull over the next stages of the project in contented relaxation.

By Friday, the repairs have all been completed, and Frits packs up his tools and goes off to do whatever the Fritses of this world have to do. We are all tired, but the feeling is rewarding. There is still one more coat of paint to be applied to the sides of the Luxor as the area above the water line also needs painting, although this is more for the looks than anything else. After all, we are going to a festival where we will all be on show, but we aren't too worried. We have the whole of the weekend to focus on giving it the beauty treatment.

I just wish I could do the same cosmetic job on my poor face. It is proving resistant to all cures except time which, in this case, is not on my side. Unfortunately too, I cannot replace my decomposing skin with new patches quite so efficiently or effectively as Koos and Frits have managed to do on the Luxor. That being said, by the time we set off for Lille next week, I should be more or less wholesome to see and nice to know again. At least I hope so.

CHAPTER TWELVE
Destination Lille

The day has arrived for our departure to Lille. Since coming off the slipway the week has been fraught with activity and preparation. The purpose of our journey is to participate in the annual *Patrimoine de Lille* festival, which Koos has been involved with since 1996. He is responsible for drumming up a 'fleet' of historic Dutch barges and other authentic pre-war tugboats to sail to Lille each year as part of a 'brotherhood of nations' style event. The boats come from all over Holland and make their way down the inland waterways through Belgium to France, ultimately gathering together on the canal just outside this border city. Then they all sail in together as a procession to moor in a small harbour in the *Bois Blancs* district, so that local people can come and experience these wonderful floating tributes to Dutch history as part of the festivities.

Owing to the intensity of the work on the slipway, there were a number of tasks related to the organisation of the event that Koos hadn't been able to complete, so the intervening days have seen him in a torment of anxious e-mailing, snail mailing and phoning. I haven't seen him half so alarmed by potentially serious crises on the water as he has been by these apparently insurmountable administration problems. You could almost see the perspiration spurting off his troubled brow, but as usual Madam Necessity cracks the whip and, even though I was pushing envelopes into the post box at the eleventh hour, it was all done in the end.

This morning we are leaving Rotterdam. It is a Saturday; it is the 8th of September and it is 7 o'clock. The sun is only just coming up. Last night, after committing Sisha into Philip's care, we moved from the Oude Haven into the Haringvliet so that we wouldn't have to disturb our neighbours or call the bridge keeper too early. As we sail quietly out of the harbour down the river with the new light outlining the buildings and glinting on the water, I realise that this is what 'the life' is about. I am feeling good anyway because my face has recovered its normal size and texture now that all the burnt skin has peeled off. Indeed, my cheeks are as soft as that baby's bottom that Mireille had in mind when she gave me the lanolin cream

Although Koos has built a small wheelhouse in a record three days to protect us from the elements, we don't need it at the moment. The weather is beautiful. The clouds scud across the brightening sky and before long we are being embraced by a warm cloak of golden light. There are a thousand images of the sun as it sparkles in the reflections of endless banks of office and apartment windows. The wind is fresh and we drink it in deeply.

Creeping through a passage behind the Van Brienenoord Island, we feel as if we are trespassing while everyone and everything is sleeping. It is so still all we can hear is the throb of the Luxor's idle engine and the lap of water against our bows.

About two hours later we reach Dordrecht, where we cross the wide stretch of the Oude Maas. At this time on a weekend morning, the busiest waterway crossroads in Europe is relatively quiet; we manage to make it straight to the entrance of the city's Wolvevershaven without any nerve-shattering close calls. As we tie up, it seems unreal to realise that this section of our journey would normally take a mere twenty minutes by train. I feel as if we have already travelled to a foreign country.

We have to stop for a while to do some shopping, and I am about to experience Dordrecht for the first time. This is funny because, although it is so close, I've never been here before and it is a real revelation. It's such an unexpectedly beautiful town. Winding, narrow cobbled streets with wonderful 16th century Dutch warehouses standing locked between tall, graceful town residences. Canals, little hump-backed bridges; in fact, everything that combines to characterise Dutch charm and history is here. I love it, and the harbour itself is pretty too, with a picturesque double drawbridge at its entrance. It is just off the main waterway but once inside, it is peace and tranquillity incarnate. The English meaning of the word 'haven' comes readily to mind.

The shopping accomplished, we loosen the ropes and cast off to continue on our way. Proceeding with all the speed our meagre 25 horses will allow us means around 9 kilometres per hour in real terms. As this is not frighteningly fast it seems to take us an age to make any real headway against what is now a fast running current, a journey made even slower by the fact that the weather has changed dramatically. By the time we reach the Hollandsch Diep, there is a Force 8 gale blowing. Remembering our last encounter with this huge stretch of water, it seems to look even more suspiciously like the sea. Worse still, in these conditions it is behaving in much the same way as an ocean. At least that's what my sudden onset of anxiety neurosis is telling me.

We have to cross to the opposite shore, which I'm convinced has vanished and we will never see again, engulfed by floods and fog. As we try to make our way out into the open water the wind is howling, and it feels as if we are barely moving at all. We *are* creeping forward, but have to fight against the strengthening current as well as the gale and progress is heart poundingly slow. It is almost impossible for both of us to stand together in the tiny wheelhouse but I don't want to be alone inside, and staying out in the open would be suicidal, so I huddle as close to Koos as I can. One side of me is soaked through. I feel like a split personality, one of which is distinctly soggy, miserable and decrepit; the other has retreated into suspended animation.

At last, after an hour, we can see the shore close to the lock that we are heading for. By now the force of the wind is driving the rain horizontally and the only discernible direction we are taking is towards the rocks I can see on our port side. The poor Luxor is taking quite as much of a battering as my nerves, as the waves hurl themselves at us. The barge's hull shudders against the assault. Gulping down my trepidation, I ask Koos what will happen if the engine gives up.

"Well," he says, still peering ahead through the driving rain, "I suppose we'll end up on those rocks. We'll lose the ship of course," he finishes matter-of-factly.

I wish I hadn't asked.

Needless to say I am almost blubbering with relief when we finally see the entrance to the first lock. But the relief evaporates in a flash. We haven't been through it yet and this is the first time I've had to help tie up in such terrible conditions. As the Luxor leaves the raging inferno of the Diep and crawls slowly through the lock gates, I lurch my way up to the foredeck, hoping Koos hasn't noticed that I am swinging from one bout of panic to the next. It won't do much for the image of cool competence that I've been practising so hard to achieve if he sees the gibbering wreck I've become. I have to focus now on tying up, so I need to get a grip on things.

Of course, the inevitable happens and the looped end of the rope I throw refuses to hook itself over the cleat in the lock wall that I need to use. The wind blows us away from the side and I'm left hurling a useless rope into oblivion, my arms flapping pathetically as it flops into the water. The next moment we are being flung back against the wall, and the subsequent bang practically has me overboard. Luckily Koos manages to get a rope fastened this time, no thanks to me, and with the stern fixed in place he can bring the bows close enough for me to slip the rope easily over the cleat and tie up. I'm feeling a trifle sheepish by now, but at least we're safe. No points for the first mate this time though.

Once through, we meet up with some other Lille-goers, including Jitze and Manette who are good friends of Koos's. They own a strong, muscular tugboat called Eems (pronounced 'aims'), and they have this wonderful idea of coupling us up to their boat the next day so that we can make better progress across the rest of the high seas we have to negotiate. We spend a turbulent night at the jetty just past the lock. It is very open and bleak here and there is nothing to break the path of the gale that is determined to force all living things under cover.

In the morning, the wind is still extremely strong and the waves metres high – only a slight exaggeration. We are therefore very pleased to get this part of the journey over with some powerful assistance from the 200 horses the Eems keeps locked up in its big Brons engine.

The weather is in fact lousy the whole day, so I am very happy to have 'work' to do inside the Luxor, making it more homely. Poor Koos decides to make use of this 'free-wheeling' time to sort things out on deck as we left with everything still largely in disarray from all the work he did before our departure. In his yellow oilskins, he is doing a very good impression of a drowned myopic canary as I watch him from the safety of the hold.

Passing through Antwerp is perhaps the most memorable sight this stormy afternoon; the sky is completely dark, a menacing anthracite grey. From somewhere, though, rays of sunshine penetrate the cloud cover, lighting up the beautiful old buildings lining the river and shining off the steeples of Antwerp's magnificent cathedral and churches. The effect is dramatic and stunning.

In a lock among the maze of harbours and waterways that criss-cross the city, we moor up next to a Belgian commercial barge. Koos starts chatting to the French speaking skipper, who seems a lively and charming little man, and we part company with plenty of good bonhomie. He is also apparently impatient to be on his way, because as the lock begins to open his barge shoots forward at an alarming speed, and he only just manages to make his exit without careering into the gates. Everyone else in the lock almost audibly holds their breath as they watch him rush through with only a hair's breadth to spare.

With another drama narrowly avoided we continue on our way, still comfortingly attached to our chunky tugboat escort. By evening, though, the skies are clearing, and we pull into a small harbour at a place called Temse. To our surprise we find our Belgian friend has tied up there for the night too.

As we pull in, the fact that we are coupled up to the Eems means we are just a just a tad too wide and, to my horror, we make rather strong contact with the Belgian skipper's precious *spits*. Although I am there clutching my rubber fender and trying to ward us off, it is all too much. The fender breaks under the strain, leaving us to scrape noisily along our neighbour's shining paintwork.

Oops. All of a sudden, small Belgian skipper is no longer full of bonhomie. In fact, in true Gallic style, he is hopping up and down, arms flailing and cursing at me very volubly – in French of course. He is not a happy chappy, and I am rather thankful I don't know what he is saying. It seems that he believes I am personally responsible for our untimely contact and that I should be the subject of his most virulent venom. Being the brave soul I have become in the past forty-eight hours, I smile and nod at him weakly, waving the remaining piece of rope that is now minus its fender in an attempt to prove that it is really not my fault. What else can I do?

Once we have moored up ourselves, Koos and Jitze nobly go and grovel, armed with bottles of strong liquor and Manette's homemade preserves. Luckily this seems to do the trick, as the gesticulating stops and the diminutive bargee is wreathed in smiles again. I suspect it is the alcohol that does the trick.

Apparently the vessel is his father's, and he is terrified that Daddy will blame him for any damage. Judging by the reckless way he left the lock in Antwerp, I am not too surprised by his parent's concern. Still, I am very glad I am no longer under threat of death and destruction, and am even more glad to have a peaceful night's sleep without being battered by wind and waves at our mooring, the way we were the night before. As I pass into an exhausted slumber I am quite convinced that my baptism is now complete, and I am already looking forward to a new day of calm waters, sunshine and pastoral serenity.

The next morning brings bright blue skies and the glowing light of early autumn. We have coffee and rolls with Jitze and Manette as, so far, we have no kitchen facilities on board. Installing the fittings for cooking with bottled gas was one of the jobs Koos intended to do before we left but, as with most barge owners, he found that everything takes longer in practice than it does in theory. The time it took to finalise all the other preparations stretched out and somehow it was the one job on the list that kept being relegated to second or even third place. Eventually, it was shelved to be 'done on the way' but with the appalling weather we've had, there has been no chance to even think about it. Maybe he will do it later.

Once we reach the relatively kindly waters of the Schelde, we uncouple from the Eems. It feels good to be under our own steam again, and this waterway to Ghent is very lovely. The river twists and winds along the lush, tree-strewn countryside with its gently rolling landscape. There are fantastic old factory buildings and warehouses on the water's edge and, although flurries of showery rain catch us now and then, most of the time we can bask in the soft air and warm sun with the roof off the little wheelhouse. Even our little mascot toy bunny, which has survived all the gales and storms in its place on the engine room, begins to dry out and look smug.

Jitze and Manette have sailed off ahead of us, but all the same it is blissful to be here, almost alone on the river and passing through such tranquil scenery. Koos offers me a spell at the wheel and I manage to feel quite relaxed as I steer a steady course along the main channel. However, the clouds are gathering again by the time we reach the Ghent 'ring' canal some fifty or so kilometres from the point where we were set free. The *ringvaart* acts as a water by-pass to the city, and here we meet up with the Eems again. We also find a graceful and very authentic *tjalk* named the Hoop op Welvaart, owned by Rotterdam friends Jan and Jacqueline, who are to be travelling companions for a short part of the journey. After chatting to them we decide it would be fun to take the small side canal and go into Ghent for the night.

The Eems has to stay put, because it is too cumbersome to navigate the narrow bends easily, so the rest of us push on to the small lock that leads into the city centre. For a while we have to wait for the lock keeper, which proves to be very tricky as there is a strong wind blowing, and during the manoeuvre to position ourselves ready for the gate to open we are twice blown hard against the wall. I feel ashamed as I am never where I should be to fend things off, and I begin to feel like a rabbit in panic as I dash from point to point trying to see where and what we are likely to hit next. Koos's mouth settles into a rigid line of disapproval as I allow his poor Luxor to take its second beating.

Eventually the lock keeper arrives and, trauma over, we pass through and proceed to the heart of the city, mooring up in a wide basin surrounded by elegant old houses nestling against each other with their feet in the water.

Ghent has to be the Venice of the north. It is stunning. Ancient and gracefully shabby, it exudes the artistic gentility of the Renaissance with a genuine Latin quality. I fall in love instantly. Beauty eclipses humanity and Koos is briefly forgotten as I promise myself I will return for a much longer stay, with or without him.

We start making moves to prepare food, but Koos's struggle to install the gas is set to become another saga as he attempts to find vital but lost parts in what I affectionately term the 'Luxor triangle'. It is too dark to make any headway so, without Manette there to look after us, Koos gives in to the demands of his stomach and takes me out for dinner in Ghent.

Despite Jitze's gentle nagging that Koos is neglecting me at a fundamental level by failing to provide a cooking fire, I am not sorry we are forced to eat out tonight. Dinner is a real treat as we have *waterzooi*, a local stew crammed full of vegetables and, in my case, chicken. Koos has seafood with his and it is all exceptionally mouth-watering. We meander back to the Luxor through the wet Ghent evening, tracing forgotten, secluded alleyways and enjoying the gleam of city lights reflected in the spreading puddles in the roads.

The next morning, after a dreamless and blissful sleep, Koos sets to work on the gas again. He has some success as the 'triangle' generously delivers up some much-needed tools. In fact, he has almost finished when a call comes from our companions, Jan and Jacqueline; they want to meet up with another ship that has now reached the Ring. Downing tools, we are off again. Luckily we've had coffee at the local bakery, as we still have no means to make our own. All the same, I am not amused that we have to leave so peremptorily, and this time it's my mouth that looks suspiciously like a rat-trap.

Seeing the small black cloud lurking over my brow, Koos springs into avoiding action and arranges via the ship's radio that Jacqueline will brew coffee for us, which we can collect from them *en route*. Wondering quite how we are going to do this, I resign myself for the moment to casting off and moving on.

Our route takes us along the incredibly winding Leie River, which is difficult to navigate at any time. Owing to the current, the silt builds up on the inside of the bends, which makes going aground a constant risk. Nonetheless, we are some way along when we hear the call that coffee is ready, and quite soon we see our friends have stopped up ahead. Pulling up alongside them, I repeat my rabbit run with a small tyre, anxiously and needlessly concerned about scratching their immaculate paintwork. They have huge inflated fenders and tyres all the way round their *tjalk* and especially at all the vulnerable spots. They are old hands at this business, and nothing I can do with my paltry little rubber ring is going to do any good at all.

Leaning over the gap, Jacqueline passes a pot over to us full of rich, ready-made, real hair-on-your-chest coffee. Absolute heaven. This is certainly the best way I know to re-fuel.

With the pleasantries over, the Hoop op Welvaart pulls away and we are left to potter along on our own again. The river's curves, oxbows and bends increase in size and extremity, and they are overhung with willow trees and dense foliage, making it very difficult to see ahead. We come to one place where the course is particularly narrow and the bend makes almost a complete circle as it turns back on itself. A house built on the outermost edge of the curve can actually be seen from all four sides.

Koos calmly asks me do the steering at this point so, not wishing to expose myself as the coward I am, I take the wheel and start turning. The sweat is pouring off me when I finally haul the whole twenty-two metres of the Luxor safely round to the other side. I glower at Koos. That was not fair.

Our next stop is a quaint little lock at a dot on the map called Astene. We moor up next to another barge that lives there with its owner, Lucas, a delightful Belgian who is also a good friend of Koos's. He is all smiles and generosity with unaffected charm and overflowing hospitality. He invites us in for coffee, and I am enchanted. The interior of his ship is my dream come true – a beautiful mix of perfection and informality, with its white paint against polished beams and brass. The table is covered with red and white checked gingham. Apparently, Lucas worked solidly for a year to convert the barge into it present state. Looking round with immense pleasure, I feel it was worth every minute.

While we have coffee out of thick stoneware mugs we hear with horrible incongruity about the attacks on the World Trade Centre in New York. It is the 11th of September 2001, a day none of us will ever forget. Shocked and numbed by the calamity, our mood is instantly dampened, but despite this I feel I will remember our meeting with the warm, friendly Belgian as one of the highlights of the trip.

We spend quite some time chatting, albeit in a subdued fashion, and Lucas shows us round the lock keeper's house, which he now runs as a small waterways museum-cum-cafe during high season. He is justly proud of the work he has done to preserve the local heritage.

Eventually we decide we need to push on and see how far we can go before nightfall. We take our leave with a certain reluctance, but not before having the compulsory *biertje* with the lock keeper.

The next stretch of canal we pass along will linger forever in my mind's eye. With the light fading, we fare towards Kortrijk with virtually no traffic to disturb the peace, other than the occasional cargo barge slipping quietly by. I stand up in the bows of the Luxor and listen to the silence. It is broken only by the gentle throb of the engine, seemingly far away to the rear, and the soft rippling of the water against the prow. The sky turns pink, and the trees on the bank become black statues against the dimming horizon. The air is sweet with the scent of freshly mown grass. It is both restful and magical. Indeed, it seems impossible to believe that across the Atlantic Ocean slaughter and carnage have obliterated any hope of peace, ever, for thousands of distraught souls.

At Kortrijk, we finally tie up to our dearly familiar friends on the Eems. It is around nine o'clock and, after sharing our stories over a beer with them, Koos and I go into a deserted town for some coffee. Everyone is home watching the news from New York, so we have the coffee bar to ourselves, along with the undivided attention of the charming waiter. He probably wishes he was home too so, affected by thoughts of what has happened, we go back to the Luxor and retire for the night.

The next morning, Koos finally finishes installing the gas. This is such an event worth celebrating that we walk into the town for a cappuccino, although in Belgium this means whipped cream instead of steamed milk, much to my dismay. Kortrijk is charming but far more upmarket and affluent than Ghent, and we take some time to wander the streets, looking in shop windows where the goods are not priced. I suppose the attitude is that if you need to know, you can't afford it. We set off again quite late, leaving Jitze and Manette, who have decided to stay on in the city a little longer. Maybe they cherish dreams of priceless grandeur.

Our day's faring is uneventful this time, barring the fact that we cross the French border, an excitement in itself. We had hoped to pass through the first of the French locks at Quesnoy-sur-Deûle before they closed for the night, but the French believe in keeping to a normal working day and when they say they close at 7:30, they really mean you have to be through and out the other side by then. Given that the whole procedure takes about fifteen to twenty minutes, and as we are only approaching the gates at 7:20, they won't let us in. We have to turn back and find somewhere to moor for the night close by.

The only possible spot is a small marina for even smaller boats at Quesnoy-sur-Deûle itself. It has flimsy floating wooden jetties with nothing but a few paltry hooks, but there isn't anywhere else. It will have to do. Koos steers the Luxor neatly across the ends of the two wooden jetties and I, in a rare fit of bravery, jump off the ship onto one of them with rope in hand and tie it proudly round a hook to prevent the Luxor from hitting the end wall. That this is the wrong thing to do, and Koos actually wants to move up to the wall, in no way dispels my pride at having momentarily overcome my fear of jumping gaps. I am pleased as punch with myself.

The village of Quesnoy-sur-Deûle is unremarkable, although the local tourist office makes much of its attractions on a grand notice board for visitors at the marina. They extol the delights of the modern housing estate, and the walking and horse riding facilities. I start musing about what I could do if I had a horse on board, as you do. In point of fact the village has nothing to offer the passing sailor at all, but we have to give them credit for trying. After an evening stroll through this eminently forgettable metropolis we cook our very first meal on the Luxor courtesy of the newly installed gas bottles; this is much more memorable. "What a treat!" We smile at each other. "What a gas!" The smiles are sheepish, but we can't help giggling.

The following morning we are off at the crack of dawn to be at the lock gate when it opens. It is still dark as we approach, and the green lights indicating that we may go in glow like the eyes of a sinister monster in the gloom. As we enter I am surprised to see the height of the walls. This is the first time I have experienced a significant difference in the water levels on each side of a lock. In Belgium, the rise or fall was barely more than a couple of metres, but at this lock the ascent is a good five metres. This means tying the rope to a hook way above our heads, which I have to reach by climbing a ladder set in to the lock wall. Feeling acutely conscious of my courage (or lack of it), I loop the rope over my shoulder and scale the slippery rungs of the ladder until, with relief, I reach the top, scramble onto safe ground, and fix the rope to a bollard. Watching from the wall I am amazed to see that by the time the water has stopped flowing in, I can simply step onto the deck. A few metres doesn't sound much, but when you see the water rising in a lock it suddenly looks very impressive.

Our first port of call is for breakfast croissants in Wambrechies, a small town just a few kilometres beyond the border, and again I am amazed at Koos's ability to tuck the Luxor, which now seems huge, into a tiny harbour on the waterfront. I perform my now customary rabbit impressions as I scamper up and down the *gangboorden* in a feeble attempt to prevent contact with the tupperware boats that line the marina walls. There is no need, however. Koos is at his masterful best in these situations, and steers us safely into a spot where we can stay for an hour or so.

It is such a pleasure to be walking through a French town when it is just waking up. The French are exceptionally good at making mornings pleasant with the smell of freshly baked bread wafting on the air, while the small cafes and bistros welcome early risers with the equally tempting aroma of fresh coffee. Everyone greets us with a cheery *bonjour,* leaving us feeling ridiculously happy with our lot.

Caffeine levels restored, we move on. With equal expertise Koos extracts us from the marina and, within a short time, we are noticing buildings and signs that speak of the outskirts of Lille. Before we reach the city, though, Koos has something special in store for me.

Turning left across the water, we slip into the Canal de Roubaix. As soon as we are a few metres into it, I know that this is the waterway I have been dreaming of ever since I got the barge habit. It is narrow and meandering, ambling its unhurried way through quiet scenery, past people's back gardens and alongside old factories. Sadly, it is now largely disused, so only one lock remains open to serve the barges that take molasses to a local yeast factory.

The lock is only just wider than the Luxor and not even twice as long, but it is fully automated in a Heath Robinson kind of way. To operate it, we have to press a button on a switch suspended on a cable that hangs from a wire, which itself is stretched over the water as you approach the lock. With one press, the gates open; the boat can move in; and we can wait for the lock to fill up before it lets us out the other side. Do-it-yourself, French style.

We continue another couple of kilometres further, waving at anyone and everyone we see. The people on the towpath seem to be just as pleased to wave back at us, too. Some distance further on we pass the yeast factory and, just beyond it where the canals widen out to accommodate a weir and another lock, we have to turn round and go back, as unhappily this one is out of use and we can go no further. Nevertheless, there are plans to re-open the entire length of the canal, and a good deal of EU money is being invested in the project. That trip will be very high on our wish list in the future.

On the way back, we stop for a couple of hours to relax and do a couple of tidying up jobs before going on into Lille. The afternoon is hot, still and peaceful and we feel very French having our after lunch rest.

The final stage into Lille doesn't take very long once we are back on the main canal. The last lock has a seven metre difference in levels, meaning that this time Koos climbs up the lock wall to tie our rope to a bollard at the top. I have suddenly metamorphosed from a rabbit into a chicken, and decide I cannot do this one.

However, it is only a matter of half an hour before we moor on a stretch of water by the Bois de Bologne on the outskirts of the city. We find that some of the other participants of the festival are already here. During the course of the afternoon and evening others arrive and, by the morning of the following day, we have the full complement of ships gathered in the area, ready to make a processional entrance into the harbour at Bois Blancs that same afternoon.

Unfortunately, but understandably, the main festivities for the Lille festival have been cancelled out of respect for the tragedy at the World Trade Centre, but the locals are still keen to see the boats; they look forward to the arrival of the Dutch 'fleet' every year. For me, however, arriving in Lille is the end of the adventure. It has been a wonderful, exciting week and I have never felt quite so alive – even when I have been scared half to death.

One point has been brought forcefully home to me, though, and that is the fact that you see the world from a totally different perspective on the water. It is another way of life entirely, and has a gentleness and timelessness you lose touch with on land. There was so much that was new for me during this trip, and I know the impressions and images I have gained on the journey through Belgium and into France will remain in my memory long after the names and places have been forgotten. If anything, and impossible as it might seem, I am more hooked than ever before.

More importantly, I am determined that I am now going to renew the hunt for my own barge with increased vigour.

The Vereeniging, the author's barge

CHAPTER THIRTEEN
Loss And Gain

After spending the festival weekend in Lille I leave Koos to travel home alone. Work calls. I cannot leave my students without guidance, and Koos needs none that I can give him, so we agree that I should take the train back to Rotterdam. In three and a half hours I am back at the place it has taken me eight days to journey away from. This is a strange and dislocating feeling, as the week on the water has been something of a time warp. I have been living with the sensation of having travelled hundreds of kilometres and of having spent an entire lifetime in a parallel universe.

It takes me a day or two to re-adjust. Sisha shows her displeasure over my absence by ignoring me completely and swishing her tail in contemptuous dismissal whenever she sees me watching her. On the first night of my return she goes out and doesn't come home until breakfast time. I fear that despite Philip's care and attention she has become increasingly feral, and I wonder how long she will stay with me.

As the days pass I fall back into the usual routines, and my experiences of life on the waterways begin to assume a mantle of fantasy as I cast my mind back to individual events and impressions. People on the quay catch me smiling at remembered images and snatches of conversation. They nod and wave back thinking they are the object of my attention, but that's fine. A smile is never wasted.

One afternoon I am sitting on the hatch of the Hoop's engine room, watching Sisha hunt early autumn leaves up and down the *gangboorden*. Philip emerges from his wheelhouse and steps over from his barge. Greeting me with teeth and eyes, he perches on the hatch cover next to me.

"I'll be working on the Hoop next week, Val," he says, scooping Sisha up to give her protesting form an enforced cuddle. "I'm going to make the windows in the top of the hold and do some other repairs, and then after that, the broker will start advertising it seriously."

This is my cue to get busy. He doesn't actually ask if I am looking elsewhere, but the message is gently clear. It's time I stepped up my efforts to find my own barge. Sighing, I wish I could make an offer on the Hoop myself, but I know I can't afford it – or, even if I could, I wouldn't have the money for the conversion. In the evening I start up the computer and open some of the sites I've looked at before, but there's nothing that appeals to me in a price range I can even contemplate. When Koos is back I'll ask him to put the word out to his Internet newsgroup. They are a diverse collection of skippers and other interested parties, and they communicate about anything and everything nautical, so if anyone knows what could be lying in wait for me, it will be them.

In the meantime I focus on preparing for my work and trying to find some kind of balance again in my everyday life. I continue to sweep and wash down the decks, and I give the wheelhouse a light sanding and another coat of varnish to protect it against the harshness of the winter weather. I have put so much work into it already I could not bear to see it deteriorate, even if the Hoop is going to be sold. That being said, the tiny interior in the *roef* has become so much my home in the last nine months, I find it hard to imagine living anywhere else now.

Thus employed, the days pass peaceably enough. Friends and harbour dwellers greet me and ask about the trip. Inevitably we discuss the devastating events of 9/11, as it has already come to be known, and I describe where we were when the news broke. It already seems like a lifetime away, but the horror of that day and the international response to it seem a lot closer and much more immediate now I'm back in the city. I can't say it is more real; life on the waterways was as up close, as intense and as personal as it can be, but here in Rotterdam the external world assumes greater importance and the consciousness of being at one with a more natural environment withdraws again into a secondary existence.

The weekend before Koos returns, I lose Sisha. There is an inevitability about her disappearance that I have felt coming for some months. She has been staying out for ever-longer periods and has objected strongly to being kept in at nights, something I have tried to do since she decided to spend one away. Nevertheless, on this particular Sunday morning she wakes me at around six in the morning. It is still dark, but her need seems to be urgent. She is standing on my bed clawing desperately at the porthole above me and yowling frantically.

Thinking it strange, but unwilling to leave her in distress, I undo the brass catch and pull open the window. She leaps out as if in answer to some primeval call, and dashes off. By the end of the day she has not returned, and in my heart I know she is not going to – ever.

The following morning my fears are further confirmed as her bowl remains untouched and, despite several walks around the harbour and its surroundings, I can find no trace of her. What is even stranger is that a young Polish man who has been helping out around the yard, and who I have often seen making a fuss of Sisha, has also gone. Perhaps this is just coincidence but when I think of the urgency with which she left, I can't help wondering. Maybe she has decided life with a rover is more attractive than being a ship's cat, and she has gone with him on his travels.

I don't like to dwell on the other possibility, although I find myself watching the water around the quays in constant dread.

Whatever the case, she has left a gap that is hard to fill, and when Koos sails into his berth in the harbour, it is a disconsolate soul he finds awaiting him.

He has had a good couple of weeks faring, especially as for some of the time his son Sanne was with him and they made a detour south and east to Valenciennes. Koos sent me a postcard with a charming black and white drawing of the old city that arrived here the day before he did. He too is sad that Sisha has gone, especially now I no longer have visits from the dogs either. They have recently moved to another harbour with my ex-husband so, other than in exceptional situations, I am not likely to see them.

In an effort to cheer me up, Koos describes places we could explore together that make me long to cast off the ropes and roam through Belgium and France indefinitely. Not very practical, but incredibly appealing.

I tell him about the increased need for me to go barge hunting again and we discuss the possible avenues of further investigation. He agrees that sending word out to his newsgroup could well bear fruit, but first I must decide what I am looking for. After spending ten days on the Luxor I have seen the advantages of the simple construction, but it is too big for me and too high. I feel uncomfortable steering when I cannot see the bows at all. Nonetheless, something similar would suit me well – scaled down somewhat and with a lower construction on top, it could be just right. The idea of having a kind of sister ship to Koos's barge is also quite tempting.

The message goes out that I am looking for a motor barge, preferably one that has space for accommodation and similar in style to a *dekschuit*. Within forty-eight hours one of Koos's long-time friends writes back with some exciting information and a photo of an absolutely charming small barge.

It is a *pakschuit*, which would probably be described in English as a local package delivery barge. It is long and narrow and shaped like a banana. It has removable panels along each side of the hold, but it has no *gangboorden*, so crossing from front to back means walking over the top of the hatch boards, rather than along the side. In a sense it is rather similar to an English Narrow boat. The steering position is horizontal, just like the Luxor's, and it has a heavy loading mast that gives it a rather serious air.

Apparently it has been well restored, and has an engine that is a monument in itself, being an ancient single cylinder hot bulb type from the early 1900's. However, it is in full working order and that gives me optimism.

The asking price is very affordable, mainly because it is totally empty and everything has to be done to convert it for living. I love the picture of this elegant and dainty barge instantly. It is a real *damesschip* and looks as if it was made for a lady. I clamour to have the address so that I can go and see it at its mooring in Grave, a small town just south of Nijmegen in the east of the country.

Koos immediately writes back to his friend asking for further details, and within days we have an appointment to go and look at it. However, I must contain my impatience for a few weeks, as the owner has asked for our understanding in waiting until his wife's condition has stabilised following an operation. As she is still in hospital, he spends most of his time there every day and cannot see his way to focusing on the sale of the barge for the time being. I can and do sympathise, and any concerns I might have had that someone else would find it first are quelled as he assures us that we will be the first to see it.

In the meantime, I keep my ears and eyes open for other options, but the more I look the more convinced I become that the little barge in Grave is the most likely choice. I have to consider the need for a permanent mooring in Rotterdam and, if I want to stay in the Oude Haven, my barge has to be authentic. Nothing else I see even comes close and would require extensive revision and restoration before being accepted, however tastefully the modernisation has been done.

The day finally dawns for the visit to Grave. It is now mid-October, and the morning bites with the hint of frosts to come. The sky is clear, though, and a thin film of mist hovers above the endless stretch of unrelieved horizon we head towards. It is like driving over a giant football pitch, every bit as green and every bit as flat. All the same, it has a mysterious beauty as land merges into sky at a vanishing point so distant it could be at the world's end.

The journey is a hundred and sixty kilometres, and takes us about two-and-a-half hours. We are due there at 10.30, and thankfully we drive into the outskirts of Grave with about ten minutes to spare. Our route description is good for once, and the road signs say what they are supposed to, so we feel rather proud as our little Renault punctually crunches up the driveway to the riverside property where the barge is moored, precisely at the designated time.

We are met by a tall, gracious old man with charming manners. He offers us coffee to warm ourselves after the long trip and we gratefully accept. Making it himself in his large, well-equipped kitchen, we realise that this is a home of ease and comfort in which money is most definitely not wanting, but poor Siem is lonely and bereft. He tells us his wife will never come home again, and the sadness in his eyes belies the acceptance of his speech. This is one of the reasons he is selling the barge, as he no longer has the time or energy to devote to its restoration and maintenance and he is worried that it will deteriorate if left neglected. When we explain where we have come from, Siem is delighted. The Oude Haven is known countrywide as the largest and most prominent of the historic harbours so, if I buy it, his little barge could not be going to a better place as far as he is concerned. I grin to myself on hearing this. I am already a favoured contender if I'm to believe what I'm hearing.

With coffee and formalities over, it is time to look at the object of our journey. We troop outside and round to the back of the house, where we are joined by a small, neat man who introduces himself as Frans, Siem's handyman. He leads the way down through the extensive garden to the river's edge. There is a wooden jetty fixed to the river bank and, tied up alongside, is the barge.

I take one look at its nameplate, and recognition floods over me. I know that this was meant to be.

While I was living and working in Johannesburg, I frequently visited a town on the southern edge of the Witwatersrand, South Africa's economic heartland. Its name was Vereeniging, and I used to enjoy the days I spent there as it was an unexpectedly peaceful place. After a morning visiting clients I would go to the park, sit under a tree in the sunshine with a book and an apple, and pass a very contented hour or so. The memory is one of stolen moments away from the frenetic bustle of life in the big city, the result being that I was very fond of the place.

Now, standing on a jetty in the east of the Netherlands on a bright cold morning in October, thousands of kilometres from its source, I see the name Vereeniging in glossy black painted letters on the bows of this lovely old barge. I have never seen it on another boat before, and even the spelling is the same as that of my South African getaway. In modern Dutch the word, which means a 'union' or 'society', has no double 'e', which is an outdated way of spelling it. However, it is still written this way in the Afrikaans language and, for me, it is most definitely like an invitation to come home.

Looking down the length of the Vereeniging I am charmed by its lean lines. Koos sees its potential immediately as, with its low profile, it can sneak through bridges that are deterrents to most of the larger sailing barges. Its narrow beam would also allow us to navigate the smaller Dutch canals whose use is mostly confined to our 'tupperware' boat friends these days. It would be fun to give them a run for their money.

Climbing down through the entrance hatch, I am immediately struck by the size of the hold. It seems very spacious compared with my living area on the Hoop, although I realise this could well be because it is largely empty. I immediately start visualising what I could do with so much room. It is a little height restricted though, and of the group standing in the centre, I'm the only one who can hold herself upright. All the others are in various positions of neck breaking contortion as they try to find some way of being comfortable without feeling too foolish. Siem and Frans are comparing notes with Koos about the history of the Dutch *binnenvaart*. Koos, who is the tallest, has his head at a full ninety degrees to his body, and is finding it difficult to give a proper account of his own waterways childhood while in this position. He looks more than slightly quizzical. I am close to irrepressible giggles as it's impossible to take anyone seriously when they are looking at you sideways.

Eventually Koos has the bright idea of squatting on his haunches and Siem props himself on the steps. Frans, who is only marginally taller than I am, makes do with bending his head over, which gives him a somewhat whimsical appearance. The three men resume their discussion about the old days of Dutch *binnenvaart*. In the meantime, I make my own tour of the interior.

There is a lot of old wood and debris piled up on the planking floor, so I cannot see what condition the bottom and sides are in, but I hear Siem telling Koos that he used to own the shipyard next door, so I am confident that he wouldn't be selling a barge that is not sound. I need to ask him about this, but at the moment I am content to browse and make an inventory of work to be done.

The iron sides of the hull have been painted grey at some point, but now they are caked and pitted with rust. It will all have to be scraped clean and painted again before being insulated and timbered. Looking up, I can see the bare hatch boards above me. They form a gentle curve over the width of the hold and are placed length ways instead of across from each side to the middle like the Hoop's. I rather like seeing them in the raw, so to speak, but realise they will have to be insulated too and covered with more appropriate ceiling panels. I am also reluctantly aware that the height will have to be increased if I take the plunge and buy it. I can manage as it is but no one else of my acquaintance would be able to stand up at all with the exception of a very few female friends who are shorter than I am.

Siem tells us that the restoration of this barge has been a labour of love for him; his father had one almost identical when he was a child. When he found the Vereeniging lying unloved and unused at a mooring in Amsterdam, he was determined to rescue it. It took him several years to convince the owners, a transport company, to part with it and he eventually acquired it four years ago. By this time the little *pakschuit* had been out of use for fifteen years and the ducks were busily staking their own claim by colonising it prolifically.

Apparently, after the former owners had stopped carrying goods with the Vereeniging in the sixties they tried converting it to a holiday boat by making some ugly modifications. Siem, however, decided to restore it to its original form. The hold had been extended to cover a large part of the foredeck, so he removed the offending protrusion and brought it back to its original length. He also made completely new hatch boards from heavy hardwood, and new panels of an authentic style replaced the louvred wooden sides between the hull and the top.

But there is more to see. Climbing back out of the hold, Siem opens up the forward hatch and we all peer inside together, our heads meeting in the middle of the opening as we jostle for position. There is quite a large space below the deck, and it is clear that at one time there were old bunk beds, as the remains of these are still in evidence. It even had a toilet fitted into the forepeak. This tickles me. I start to picture what might have happened if someone were enthroned when the barge hit something head on. After all, the Vereeniging has an impressive *berghout* or rubbing rail, made of strong hardwood, so the skipper wouldn't have been too worried about bumping into obstacles such as mooring poles or lock walls. I can just imagine the expletives and sparks issuing from the open hatchway as the poor occupant was sent flying with his trousers round his ankles. Nevertheless, there are present day possibilities suggested by these signs of previous domesticity and I realise there is space here for a 'guest room'.

We then troop onto the jetty and go to the rear of the barge to see Siem's pride and joy – the engine room.

Climbing down from the steering deck into the tiny, cramped space, Koos and I are immediately awed by the monument that sits regally before us. One huge cylinder and a monster red flywheel dominate the room. Next to it is a massive cylindrical muffler for the exhaust gas which itself is fed through a huge steel pipe to the rear of the barge. It is wow, and double wow.

It is not the engine the barge was born with in 1898, which was a paraffin-fuelled model. This one was installed in 1921 and was built by the Industrie works in Alphen aan den Rijn. Siem explains how it all works, and how the top of the cylinder housing has to be heated up by a gas burner until it is red hot. Only then can the compressed air be used to start the engine. Fed by short sharp bursts into the cylinder, the air forces the piston down, which turns the flywheel. This in turn drives the piston up and down again, thus allowing the engine to start running as the diesel fuel takes over the job of ignition. Siem says he will give us a demonstration after we have seen the *roef*. I am pleased to hear this as, although I admire such old machinery, I wonder if it is still viable.

Opposite the entrance to the engine room is another hatch-way giving access to the *roef*. One look inside and I am sold. It is tiny and far too low, even for me, but it is lined with the original cupboards and panelling and has old bench seats all round. This was where passengers sat in the days of its cargo carrying career and, despite its functionality, the woodwork and small windows are all beautifully fashioned. Siem admits that Frans has had to do a huge amount of restoration here as the steelwork was completely rotten and looked more like Bruges lace when he bought it. In turn, this meant that the old timberwork was also sadly rotten in places but now it all looks perfect. Loving fine carpentry as I do, I fall heavily for it and want it urgently, although in all honesty I can't think what I can actually do with it on a practical level.

With all these wonderful impressions overwhelming me, Koos and I stand gazing at the barge from the jetty as Siem and Frans set to work to start the engine. They have had it running earlier, so it isn't as cold as it would normally be, but even so it takes fifteen minutes before the cylinder head is warm enough to start it. The flywheel begins turning the wrong way, though, so they have to slow it down almost to a standstill and then get it moving again with another burst of diesel delivered manually by using a small lever on the fuel injection pump. This time it all goes well, and the old motor chunders into life. It makes the most wonderful sharp 'tak takking' sound, and we all spontaneously start clapping. Without needing any further encouragement, Siem briskly tells Frans to cast off the ropes, and he pulls away from the jetty to give us a brief demonstration.

The Vereeniging looks beautiful on the water: sleek, elegant and wholly desirable. I make up my mind there and then. Inefficient old engine or not, I want it and I'm going to have it. End of story.

An hour later, hands have been shaken on the deal and I tell Siem that as long as the Committee in the Oude Haven agree that I can take it there, I will buy it. I need to get their approval first, but I don't have too many concerns on that score. I am quite convinced that this little barge is almost unique and, with the added attraction of its monumental engine, I am certain of a place in the harbour. To help me, Siem gives me some photos I can show the 'yay or nay sayers' as well as a history of the barge and its engine. I rather think he wants me to have it even more than I do.

The drive home is somewhat euphoric. I am not even contemplating the work that lies ahead of me. Not yet at any rate. I am just thinking of the fact that I was destined to find this particular barge. With its name and the associations it has for me, and only me, it was inevitable. I smile to myself.

It is not quite a year since I made the decision to leave South Africa and come back to the Netherlands as an experiment. I had no clue what was in store for me then, but there is nothing like having a barge and a skipper to concentrate the mind and, between them, the Hoop and Koos have given me the confidence that I can make a go of The Life. What's more, I now know that, for the foreseeable future at least, I will have a purpose, a project and a home of my own. It is a good feeling.

CHAPTER FOURTEEN
The Beginning Of The Rest

The next few weeks are a whirl of stomach-knotting anxiety as I wait for permission to bring the Vereeniging to the Oude Haven. I have written a letter to the Director of the Foundation and enclosed a number of photos, together with an outline of a plan for the barge's further restoration. There are still things that need to be done and I am in the blessed position of having a very old photo, taken when the barge itself was new. I found it in the envelope Siem handed me, and I am touched that he should have given me something so precious.

After studying the faded sepia image closely Koos and I see that originally there was a *koekoek* over the engine room hatch in place of the flat cover that it has now. Added to this, there was a beautiful teak-wood entrance to the *roef* which has also gone and, of course, high on the priority list for replacement is the oversized steel mast that absolutely must be exchanged for a wooden one. There is therefore still plenty to keep the committee happy in terms of restoration and I have mentioned my intention to raise the height of the hold as well. Luckily, I have established a precedent for this, as in former days, when there was an extra large cargo, it was not unusual for the skipper to add additional planks to the side panels to accommodate the increased load.

The first person I go to with the news has to be Philip. I don't want him to hear from someone else that I've found my barge, so it's important that he knows before the harbour grapevine gets going. I buttonhole him on his own boat the day after seeing the Vereeniging, and show him the photos. His eyes light up with pleasure on my behalf, but for once the gleam of his smile is absent. This is serious business and I am making a weighty decision, so it is no time for mischief or teasing. He also realises something else:

"Of course this isn't such good news for me, is it Val?"

Puzzled and slightly thrown, I ask him why.

"Well," he reasons, "I haven't sold the Hoop yet, so I'll be losing a good tenant when your *schip* arrives."

It sounds like an admonishment but the twinkle in his eye belies the peevishness of his words.

"Come on, Philip," I laugh, "do you think I'm going to live in an empty hold? It'll be months before I can move on board and by that time, you'll be glad to be rid of me."

"Ah no, Val," he grins "I *am* Dutch you know and I'll never be glad to see the back of a nice bit of income." And, with a wicked chuckle, he darts away to escape the swat I am about to deliver to his left ear.

The next person to be told is Mireille. She has been my friend and confidante for so long now it would be equally hurtful for her to learn via the local gossip that I am buying my own *woonboot*. Typically, she takes the news with an unruffled calm, a smile and a promise to help with the work. I thank her but know she cannot deliver on such an offer. There is far too much to be done, and with the demands of her small baby, my friend will not have the time.

Two weeks pass, during which I try to focus on everything but images of a small, dainty barge with green and red paintwork floating across the screen in my mind. Then, at last, I have some positive feedback from the Director who says that, in principle, the Vereeniging qualifies and is welcome in the harbour. However, after it arrives it will have to have the dreaded inspection by the *schouwcomissie*, those learned and earnest men who will examine every centimetre of my new acquisition. They will have the last word in pronouncing whether I meet the criteria for a contract to stay and complete the restoration. Despite this warning, I am overjoyed, totally ignoring all the 'subject to' clauses. I'm in, and that is what's important. I'll take care of the rest later.

After happily confirming to Siem that we can go on to the next stage, I make an appointment with his *notaris*, who is the lawyer qualified to undertake the transfer of property. In the Netherlands, the purchase of floating homes is so common that they are handled in much the same way as the immovable type. The particular firm of notaries we are using is also known to be experienced in handling the sale of ships, boats and barges. As soon as the money has changed hands, we will sign the deed of sale. The register of ownership at the *Kadaster* (Deeds Office) will then be changed into my name.

On the day of the signing Koos comes with me in the event of any language problems, and we are led into a dignified boardroom with furnishings as sombre as the matters conducted within its walls. It is all very official and sober, and I have more than just a notion of the significance of what I am undertaking. The *notaris* acting for Siem is a pleasant but studious-looking woman who gives the necessary explanations about the process to underscore the weight of the transaction. I sign, she signs for Siem, and Koos signs as witness. She shakes hands with both of us when the deed is done, and then it is over. The Vereeniging is officially mine, and now all that remains is to go and fetch it.

Feeling slightly dizzy with exhilaration, we return to the harbour, but for me it is business as usual as I have to go off to work and put all thoughts of my new property aside; for the time being, at least.

The weather is turning rapidly from autumn into winter, and the beginning of December is almost upon us. It is cold, very cold, with bleak, grey, misty mornings. We have arranged to collect the Vereeniging on the last Saturday of the month. The plan is to travel to Grave on Friday evening, stay overnight and leave at daybreak the following morning.

There will be three additions to our crew as well. Firstly, and unexpectedly, I have the dogs, Polly and Daisy, for a short spell while my ex-husband is away. I cannot leave them alone or with anyone else, so they will have to come too. The other addition is my daughter Jodie, who has been much miffed at missing out on previous trips. She is not to be deterred from joining in on this one, despite the risk of exposure, frostbite and extreme discomfort.

We've also had a very kind offer from the friend who drew my attention to the Vereeniging in the first place. Given the fact that we will have no *marifoon*, or navigation lights, he has offered to meet us *en route* and escort us through the busy waters back to Rotterdam. Much as I would like to think we could do it alone, I'm quite relieved, and gratefully accept Cees's generous offer. With the old engine untried over more than a kilometre since Siem overhauled it, it is something of an unknown quantity. It wouldn't be very comforting if it were to cut out in mid-stream as the Luxor did on the Hollandsch Diep; without any means of communication the consequences are not something I care to contemplate. Even so, the butterflies are performing pirouettes around my stomach when I think of the trip ahead. After all, it's *my* barge we are talking about now, and my investment for the future.

The day arrives, and we collect Jodie from work and pile her in the back of the little Renault together with the dogs and the provisions. After the initial excitement of seeing Jo again, Polly and Daisy settle back into the somnambulant state they usually adopt in the car and leave my poor daughter struggling to find some space amongst the mixed up heap of paws and claws.

The drive east is long and slow as there are numerous *files* (traffic jams) to contend with. I am nervous with anticipation, Koos is quiet with concentration, and Jo is simply tired – so we are all rather uncommunicative for the three or so hours it takes to reach the back road approach to Grave. Siem knows we are coming but has said that he might be delayed at the hospital with his wife, so there's a chance he won't be home when we arrive. In that case, we'll have to look for somewhere to stay overnight. We won't want to bother him to find beds for us if he arrives late, added to which I haven't confessed to having the dogs with me either.

Nevertheless, the closer we get the more I hope he is there, since we are all terribly sleepy.

Sadly we are out of luck on this occasion, because as we approach the house there isn't a light to be seen. The darkness is intense and across the water to the back of the property all is stygian black. Sighing with exhaustion, we turn around and head for the highway, not knowing where we will find a place for the night – especially one that accepts dogs. Luckily, though, my daughter has not lost the bright-eyed observance that she has had since she was a child. It was sometimes an embarrassment then, but it's a blessing now. She has noticed a neon sign of a parrot near the house, meaning that there must be one of those 'chain store' hotels very close by. The parrot is famous throughout the country as a symbol of cheap accommodation and reasonable food.

It doesn't take long before we find it and I shamelessly send Jodie in to flutter her eyelashes at any male around to ask if they have room for three adults and two dogs. It sounds like a tall order to me and, despite her charms, I am not all that hopeful. Still, it seems I underestimate either her charms or her wiles, or both, because in no time she is back with a big triumphant smile on her face.

"No problem, Mum," she beams. "We can all stay and we can share a family room. There's even a bed for the dogs!"

"Jo, you're a genius," Koos and I say in unison.

"I know," my daughter grins smugly, "but it helped that there was a very nice young guy at reception when I went in. He's even given me the key already." And as if it is her final, most brilliant trick, she pulls the room key from behind her back and waves it at us victoriously.

Our mood lightens instantly and we all troop into the hotel, after ensuring the dogs have done their last business of the night. The room is standard commercial decor with two big beds and a camping stretcher under the window. This, I presume, is the dogs' bed so, taking the hotel employee at his word, I lay out their own blankets on the bare, spongy mattress and encourage them to snuggle down together. As far as it is possible for a dog to do so, Polly and Daisy positively grin at me. This is luxury indeed.

The rest of us tuck into the sandwiches I've luckily thought to bring with me. It's far too late for the kitchen to be open for food. After eating, we drink coffee made from the sachets left in the room. There is an atmosphere of adventure about us, and we are as happy as schoolchildren on a trip as we wash and climb into bed. Even so, the stresses of the day have taken their toll and, being the adults we really are, it is merely a matter of minutes before the lights are out and we are all drifting into much needed slumber in readiness for the real excitement to come.

I am awake at six the next morning, shocked rudely out of my sleep by the piercing bleep of my mobile phone which, in my pre-waking dream, is a police siren chasing me. It is a relief to be fully conscious and find nothing more threatening than a shrill, buzzing computer chip in a plastic case. Swinging my legs out of the warm comfort of the bed, I stumble into the bathroom to shower before the rest of the troops start clamouring for attention. Dressed and ready for action, I shake Jo, Koos and the dogs awake, none of whom have shown any signs of consciousness so far. Leaving the two-legged members to look after themselves, I take the reluctant quadrupeds out for a morning constitutional before leading them to the car, where I give them some food and leave them watching my departure mournfully from the back seat.

Back in the hotel room, Koos has phoned Siem and warned him of our imminent arrival. We are all hoping he will give us some coffee before we set out, as there is nothing left but tea in our room and that really doesn't do the trick so early in the morning. A good shot of caffeine is a pre-requisite for this kind of venture.

Scrunching up his driveway in the dark, we are cheered to see lights on in the downstairs rooms and, sure enough, Siem greets us with a smile and a coffee pot. Not only that, he has a plate of delicious *gevulde koeken*. These flat, slightly crisp cakes have a delicious soft almond filling and are sinfully scrumptious. Armed now with coffee strong enough to make the ears ring and with the *gevulde koeken* a satisfying presence in our stomachs, we are ready to move.

As we make our way down to the Vereeniging, Siem sees the dogs' faces peering out at us from the car. He is surprised but unfazed that they are coming with us on the trip. By now he has accepted that we are up for more or less anything, besides which my attractive young daughter is far more interesting than a pair of ageing canines. Despite his advancing years and devotion to his wife, our host is not oblivious to the appeal of a bright young thing in his midst. Not only that, he has a Master's in social skills and charm, which he clearly enjoys practising now and then. For her part, Jodie plays her role in this exercise to perfection, and the two of them are a fair way to becoming firm friends even at this unearthly hour.

The sky is beginning to lighten, but as it does so we see there is a heavy mist hanging over the land and water, and the visibility is virtually nil – slightly disconcerting given that we will have no lights on board. Still, Cees and his tugboat will be meeting us and, as long as we don't reach the busy stretches before he reaches us, we should manage.

Jodie gets the dogs comfortably installed in the *roef* while Koos helps Siem prepare the engine for starting. It takes all its customary twenty minutes to heat up the head, a process which is gauged by watching for feathery wisps of steam from the small brass decompressor on the side of the cylinder housing. Once Siem judges it to be hot enough, he checks that the air bottles he has filled the day before are still up to a full fifteen bars of pressure – the amount needed to start the engine. Fortunately they are, and his experience is now all that's necessary for the final stage as, with one jerk of the lever, the flywheel starts turning. Luckily too it is going the right way, and with this omen of good fortune we feel we can cast off the ropes and set off. Even so, we let the engine run while we say our final farewells to Siem.

He clasps my hands warmly between his. It is an emotional moment as after all, he has put a fortune's worth of love and devotion into the Vereeniging. Then, he gives Jodie a quick hug and Koos a firm handshake before stepping back onto the jetty and letting us leave.

Jo slips the ropes from the bows while I flick them from the bollards at the rear, and as we coil the lengths neatly in readiness for the lock, Koos steers us away from the side. Within moments we have pulled away from the jetty and are in the main channel; Siem is diminishing from our sight as he waves and waves until we can see him no more through the mist.

It is devastatingly cold. The world before, around and behind us is a steely grey and we can see only a matter of metres ahead. Jo and I stand shivering next to Koos and we are all talking in hushed tones; for some reason, the occasion demands it. It is a silent, still and unearthly morning but, for all that, it is strangely beautiful in an other-worldly way. The engine's sharp clapping echoes back to us across the water, a sound somehow isolated and remote from us by the time it has returned. We have a sense of being very much alone in our parallel world. That said, I can see that despite the frigid conditions Jo is enjoying it; it is tremendously romantic in an esoteric way.

No more than five hundred metres from Siem's jetty, however, we come to the first lock. Pulling slowly in, it is Jo's turn to do the rabbit run with the fender as she valiantly tries to prevent the Vereeniging from scraping along the lock wall.

"Don't worry, Jo," I feel compelled to call. "It's all wood, so nothing's going to hurt us."

"Now you tell me!" is the indignant response from the blurred shape in the gloom up front. "I've been risking life and limb up here!"

I smile at the exaggeration.

"Just get a rope on one of the hooks in the wall. Try the first one you can reach!" I shout, thinking we are in danger of going too far along the lock, but of course Koos has everything in hand. The engine is in reverse, effectively applying the brakes, and this gives me time to throw a loop over a hook at the stern end of the barge.

As we move backwards I can fasten the line as a 'spring', and then clamber forward to help my poor confused Jo, who has managed to get one end on the wall but doesn't know where to fix the other on the deck.

"Where do I tie it, Mum?" Her call is desperate, and she is waving the rope at me as if it's some kind of venomous snake she's trying to control. Rescue is urgently required.

The fact that I have to cross the top of the barge in these conditions makes it a risky venture. The tarpaulin that covers the hold is very slippery, but I manage it now without incident or even loss of dignity. Showing Jo how to make another spring, I tie the rope to the two small bollards on the Vereeniging's bows in a tight figure of eight, so that we are now firmly attached and can move neither forwards nor back. This is important as we can't switch off the engine, even though we are supposed to. Lock protocol, and so on. In our case, it would take far too long to start it again when the doors are ready to open, an argument that the official on duty grudgingly accepts.

The water level drops a couple or three metres; the doors swing slowly open; Jo and I nonchalantly flick the ropes free and then we are off again, making our way downstream along the Maas. The mist is lifting slightly and, looking over to the river bank, we see a figure waving to us. It is Siem. He has jumped in his car and is following us along the towpath. The Vereeniging's engine is beating a strong, regular tattoo and we are going steadily, so he is probably relieved to see all is well. We wave enthusiastically back.

One or two kilometres further along a bridge looms up ahead, still largely shrouded in mist. There is another figure leaning over the railing, waving to us as we approach. The details become clearer and out of the gloom, Siem emerges again. We laugh up at him as we pass under the bridge. Within two kilometres we see him yet again, this time at the end of a small spit protruding from the shore. It's beginning to be a comedy now as we wonder where he will pop up next, unexpectedly waving us on our way. But it's also rather touching. It must be a terrible wrench for him to be parting with the little barge that has consumed his interest for so long.

Jodie takes a spell at the wheel, a treat guaranteed to put a smile on her face and make her forget that the redness of her nose would challenge a certain reindeer. Koos mutters an excuse to dip into the engine room to make sure the oil pot is topped up, something that has to be done every two hours. We have not even been going for much more than one hour yet, but there's no doubt it is lovely and warm in there. Meanwhile I take a peek at the dogs, who are sensibly staying put in their nest in the *roef*. Even they show no signs of any desire to join us outside.

The mist has lifted a little more, but it still swirls and eddies around us in some kind of sensuous, frivolous dance. Every now and then one of the huge thirteen-hundred tonner commercial barges materialises as if from nothing, only to fade eerily into the fog bank behind us as it ploughs its way upstream. Then, after several more kilometres of gentle but steady progress, we realise that we have seen the last of Siem and we are all touched with sadness, wondering if he will ever see the Vereeniging again. These gloomy thoughts are thankfully short lived, though, because up ahead Koos spots the bows of what looks suspiciously like a tugboat. Pulling out his mobile phone, he punches in a number and a few seconds later, he is smiling with the confirmation that Cees and his wife will very shortly be alongside.

In fact, it only takes a few minutes before the Johanna C makes a turn in the river behind us and draws up on the starboard side of the Vereeniging. Ropes are thrown and fixed as both springs and trusses and, once the two men are satisfied that we are properly secure, I go below and turn off the Vereeniging's engine. It has done very well up to now and hasn't missed a beat, so I feel a twinge of regret that we are now being towed, something I know that Jodie shares with me as she has thoroughly enjoyed her spell as the helmsman. All the same, it is probably wise, as we will later be joining a much busier waterway and, without lights or communications in this weather, it could be dangerous.

Our progress now is considerably faster as we are pulled smoothly along by the powerful tug. Koos joins Cees and his wife in their wheelhouse but Jodie and I stay on the Vereeniging and take turns in keeping Polly and Daisy company – not that they seem too perturbed by the change of pace. As long as they are warm and comfortable, nothing much seems to ruffle them.

We also pass some time using the tug's high pressure hose to wash off some of the moss and mould that has accumulated on the Vereeniging over the winter months. Cees apparently feels a good scrubbing is mandatory despite the weather, and although I could willingly put it off until conditions are slightly more inspiring, his insistence brooks no argument.

It seems to take no time at all to arrive at the Afgedamde Maas, the connecting waterway from the

Maas to the Merwede. This is where we begin to meet much more traffic, and the waters become much choppier.

Once on the Merwede, we are on the super-highway and the huge tankers and container carriers seem to roar past with intimidating frequency, sending rolling waves towards us as their parting gift. The poor Vereeniging smacks and bashes against the side of the tugboat in an alarming fashion and, once or twice, I am soaked with spray. This is not fun anymore, and so I retreat to sit with the dogs and Jo. There is definitely both comfort and safety in numbers.

From time to time Koos pops in to bring us coffee and snacks to keep us going till we reach Dordrecht, where we are stopping for the night. Jodie will also be leaving us there, having decided that a night crammed in the *roef* with two unwashed adults and two damp and fusty dogs is probably not on her wish list of desirable experiences. I can't say I blame her.

We reach Dordrecht at around four in the afternoon, and the light is already fading rapidly. I am pleased we are here so early as it allows me to walk to the station with Jo. I can combine this with exercising my furry friends as well as stopping at the supermarket to pick up some provisions.

With Jodie thanked, hugged, kissed and dispatched at the station, I return to the harbour where we have moored up. Koos and I then pass the evening talking ships and boats and things with our escorts, until weariness overcomes us. We step over to the Vereeniging and shut ourselves into the *roef* for the night.

We have two single mattresses squashed into the triangular shape left between the benches and cupboards that surround this tiny space. We also have duvets and pillows and, somehow, we manage to arrange ourselves with a dog each at our feet as we snuggle down. Although it is icy cold outside, our four living, breathing bodies do a grand job of creating a good cosy fug and in fact, during the night, I am forced to open the windows to prevent us all from suffocating.

Nevertheless, the morning comes all too soon and, after steaming cups of coffee provided by Cees's wife, we make ready for the last leg of the journey. Much to my delight, Mireille turns up on the quayside with her family just as we are preparing to cast off. They had mentioned they would try and join us for this last part of the journey, and I am so pleased they were able to make it.

Koos and I have already decided we'd like to make a grand entrance into the harbour, which means starting the engine and going in under our own power. Once we are *en route* we start to check the air bottles and find the pressure has dropped, so we will need more air. Luckily Cees has a compressor on board. Leaving Mireille and her husband to sit with the dogs and enjoy the scenery, Koos and I busy ourselves making the preparations to start the engine.

We are complete novices though, and what looked so simple when Siem was showing us now turns out to be hopelessly complicated and frustrating. The air bottles take aeons to fill up, so that by the time we are ready to start heating the cylinder head, we are already back in Rotterdam. I have seen absolutely nothing of this last stretch of water, or my friends, closeted as I have been with my impressive hunk of cast iron.

Before we know it we are in the Haringvliet, waiting for the bridge to open into the Oude Haven. Now it is a race against time to see if we can get the engine going before the bridge keeper arrives to let us through. The tension is crackling in the engine room as time after time we try to get the flywheel turning, but whatever we do we cannot get the timing right, and we drain the bottles of air again. Eventually, Cees fixes his own air lines to our system and keeps his compressor running to maintain the pressure. Finally, with one mighty burst, Koos has the flywheel on the go and, to our exhausted relief, the engine starts just seconds before the black capped official brings the booms down across the road and slowly opens the bridge.

Exalted, exhilarated and dirty, as well as grinning from ear to ear, we uncouple ourselves from the Johanna C and Koos takes the wheel to steer the Vereeniging into the Oude Haven. With the clap of its wonderful old Industrie motor resounding across the water and echoing off the buildings, we motor into the harbour.

Friends and neighbours emerge from holds and wheelhouses to watch us make our way to the end of the row of barges. Everyone smiles hugely and claps to see this beautifully old-fashioned little barge taking its place among them. We pull slowly in next to the Hoop where other hands are there to help us with ropes, fenders and any other assistance they can give.

The Vereeniging has arrived, and a new chapter is about to begin. The Hoop, which has been my home for the last year, is a fitting neighbour to the newcomer. Being very much the 'mother ship' and *'grande dame'* of the harbour, she looks like the parent to this dainty child, but before long I will have to make the transition from one to the other and the Hoop will move on; a farewell that will be a sad one for me. It has been through this graceful barge that I've developed my love for the watery way of life. But with the Vereeniging to pour my energy and imagination into, I know the pain will be less severe.

On the other hand, I shouldn't forget that having a barge of my own will give me wonderful and endless opportunities for a whole crop of new offerings to the water gods.

Beautiful Dutch historic barges

EPILOGUE

The May sunshine burns into my skin as I sit, tired but content, on the foredeck of the Vereeniging. I am at the end of a gruelling week on the slipway; a week I hope never to experience again, even though it has been one of the most heart-warming in terms of the friendship, good will and support of my fellow *liggers*.

When I first saw the Vereeniging back in October last year I fully intended to ask Siem about the condition of the barge below the water line and assumed that he had taken care of that, being a former ship yard owner. Nevertheless, in the emotion and enthusiasm of the moment, I completely forgot to speak to him. In effect, I did something no-one should ever do: I bought a boat in the water. Cardinal sin number one, and if not that, sheer stupidity at the very least.

I began to be nervous about what I'd done when the insurance inspector first came to take a look at the Vereeniging when I applied for cover. He asked me about its maintenance history and I had to confess I didn't know.

"Hmm," was his reply. "We'll have to put an exclusion on your policy until it's been fully inspected."

I then began to see trouble at every turn. In the first months after I bought it I spent weeks in the freezing cold of the empty hold, clearing out the old and rotten floorboards and then scraping the muck of a century's use off the bottom of the hull. As I progressed I saw places along the *kimmen*, the part where the sides curve into the flat bottom, which were thick with rust. Too thick. I also saw places where the ribs of the barge's framework were totally rotten, and were only being held in place by the concrete strengthening that had been placed along the inside of the *kimmen*. Gulping inwardly, I told myself this wasn't necessarily a problem on the outside, but I was finding it hard to remain convinced as I slowly worked my way along the whole of the bottom.

Then there was the mysterious water that seemed to keep seeping in from somewhere. I couldn't see any leaks but every time I got it dry, more water would appear. I assured myself it was condensation. Must be. After all, I was working on bare iron, which itself was sitting in icy water. With a small fan heater to keep the worst of the cold off, I had to be making quantities of the stuff. Didn't I?

Every now and then I would consult one of my oracles for further reassurance. Koos agreed with the condensation theory, although I have a feeling he was just trying to help me avoid panic until I could have it properly investigated. Philip came to have a look around too, and suggested it might be coming from the engine room.

"All ships have water in the bilges, Val," he comforted me. "I've got thousands of litres in mine," he added, carelessly exaggerating as if this was all perfectly normal. Then he smiled the smile, patted me on the back sympathetically, and disappeared again.

The neighbourly brothers were next. They studied the growing puddle pensively, and decided on the condensation theory too. That made this the favourite for the time being, as Frits thought it was more likely to be rainwater finding a way in somewhere. He was doing the job of raising the height of the hold for me, which involved removing each section of hatch boards as a single unit and using a large tarpaulin to cover the open top, so his theory also seemed possible. I sighed with anxiety and frustration. As I've said before, everyone in the harbour has their own ideas and they all sound equally reliable and decisive.

Finally, the day came when I managed to get a week on the slipway. I'd promised the insurance man I would take the first opportunity for a *keuring*, but I'd had to wait till a cancellation came up, as everything had been booked for the year. Luckily someone who had reserved their spot at the beginning of May couldn't make it, so Bertus gave me the chance to take their place.

One of the first things I'd bought was a compressor to fill the air bottles, so Koos and I managed to start the engine on our own – a minor triumph for both of us. After manoeuvring the little barge to the slips, we were hoisted slowly up and, for the first time ever, I was able to take a good look at the bottom. At first sight I was relieved. It didn't look too bad at all, not even after cleaning all the mussels off with the high-pressure hose and letting it dry.

But then the insurance inspector came.

Half an hour later I escaped to work, desperate and devastated. The results were disastrous, but not entirely unexpected after my earlier investigative operations. All along the *kimmen* he had taken his hammer and tapped away until holes appeared. Several of them. The size of golf balls, mostly. The verdict was that the Vereeniging needed new steel plates to cover the rusted iron of the *kimmen* on both sides of the barge and along the entire length of the hold, a process known as 'doubling'.

Not only this, but the propeller shaft was also completely rotten and would have to be replaced. This was where the water had been coming in. With the unaccustomed use it had on the way from Grave, the grease surrounding the flange was about the only thing preventing water from pouring through into the boat, and it was astonishing that we'd kept the propeller at all. The amount of work was horrendous and almost impossible for just one week, but there was no way I could go back in the water until it was done.

When I arrived back from work, still not knowing what to do, Philip met me on the yard. He put an arm round my shoulders, gave me a hug and said, "Don't worry Val, I'll help you fix it."

The next was Frits. In his characteristically tentative way, he kindly offered to work with Philip to do the necessary 'doubling'. Then Joram the musician came and said he could do some of the patchwork too. I was overwhelmed. All these skills, and they were being pledged freely by these generous neighbours out of the kindness of their hearts. With Koos unquestioningly giving of his time and help, I had the best team possible. I could have cried with gratitude, but instead I just smiled and felt humble.

That was all just a week ago now. The days in between have been a kaleidoscope of activity, filled with intense work, laughter, camaraderie, and more work again. While my team were cutting, shaping and welding, another harbour friend, Peter, organised the new propeller shaft and fitted it; and lastly, working round them, among them and behind them, was me: I was painting, helping, cleaning up, hindering, making tea, coffee and sandwiches, running here, there and everywhere for welding rods, rollers and paint, and generally making my rabbit run with a fender look like a stroll in the park.

And now, it's all over. Unbelievably, the work is all done and the team have packed up their tools and gone on to other work and other jobs. They have been true heroes, each and every one of them, and I will never forget how they have saved the day – and my barge.

The Vereeniging is already looking slightly different. The top has been raised twenty-four centimetres along the length of the hold, and I've added pieces to all the panels to fill the gaps. At the end, where the hold meets the engine room, the extra height allows for a narrow window across the width of the barge, which I intend to keep as no one can really see it and it gives such wonderful light inside. So, with the bottom now sound and summer on its way, I can go on to build myself a proper home.

After all the stress, hard work and emotion of the past week, this moment of quiet feels good. The warmth is healing, the afternoon light is gentle and the sun glints on the ripples of the outgoing current. I can still smell the mussels that came off the bottom. They are bagged up in the skip, awaiting collection, and are beginning to be distinctly ripe, but it's fine. Even this I don't mind now.

Reflecting back on everything that has happened, I know that these experiences I have described are all part of life on the waterways. Anyone who has chosen to live and travel on a barge will have been through most, if not all, of these lessons and learning curves, and there is nothing unique about mine. Nevertheless, they are special to me, and the ways of the water with all its challenges, and all the wonderful people who live on it, have enriched me greatly. I cannot think that I will easily exchange it now for one of land based ease and convenience.

THE END

Additional information

Thank you so much for reading my book. I have deliberately chosen not to include many photos in these pages as it makes the book more expensive to produce.

For those interested in seeing photos of the harbour and the barges, I have a selection on a page in my blog, which you can find here:
http://vallypee.blogspot.nl/p/watery-ways.html

Or here on Flickr:
https://www.flickr.com/photos/29479087@N04/albums/72157690293872862

So do click on these links and take a browse through the images.

About me

I was born in London, England, and grew up in both north London and the west of Dorset. After completing my degree in English, History and French at Bournemouth, I took a further course in the conservation and restoration of museum artefacts at Lincoln College of Art.

I then spent two years doing furniture restoration before going to South Africa in 1981 with my husband and small children. However, I left South Africa permanently in 2001 and have settled in the Netherlands, where I share my time between my barge in Rotterdam and a cottage in Zeeland. I teach academic and business English on a freelance basis and write in my spare time.

More books by Valerie Poore

I have written several other memoirs. The sequel to this book is Harbour Ways, which I first published in 2014. My other memoirs are as follows:

African Ways: Recollections of life in South Africa (2011)
African Ways Again: More recollections of life in South Africa (2018)
Highveld Ways (2019)
Walloon Ways (2015)
Faring to France on a Shoe (2017)

I have also written two novels:
The Skipper's Child (2012)
How to Breed Sheep, Geese and English Eccentrics (2013) (although I should mention this is part memoir as it is heavily based on my years as a smallholder in England before moving to South Africa, even down to the names of the animals)

All my books are available on Amazon, worldwide. The link to my author page on Amazon.com is:
https://www.amazon.com/Valerie-Poore/e/B008LSV6CE/

Printed in Great Britain
by Amazon